WHAT OTHERS HAV̲ _ . ̲ ̲ ̲ ̲
ABOUT THE BOOK

I love the Reality (Questionnaire) tests you incorporated into your book.

I have known Michael for over 15 years and watched him grow amazing companies. From Electrical, Fire, Data and AC Trade Services to an online air conditioning business, nutrition and an extremely successful online health and fitness company. I am so happy he has finally shared his methodology with the world.

Recognising the One Thing you have to get right before attempting to grow your business is genius. I would urge you to start your wealth conditioning program ASAP!

- **Ian Marsh, author of The Inconvenient Truth about Business. CEO - Streetsmart Business Consultants**

In my position, I read many books about business – all I can get my hands on. Some are great, most are mediocre, and few actually say anything radically different. That is until Michael wrote this book. This isn't just another business book.

This actually raises awareness and works on the single biggest barrier to any business's success – the business owner. This shows them what is holding them back and what to do about it, and once they have the correct mindset, the book covers exactly what to do to take their business to a whole new level, one they have probably never dared dream was possible.

- **Andrew Carter, author of the Rhino Retailers and Authority & Influencer Marketing**

I love a book with real action steps that are easy to implement; this book is it! This book is a holistic guide for business owners looking to fast-track their success and growth personally and professionally. Michael is sharing exactly how to break through the challenges as you grow your business. If you follow the steps in this book, you will have immediate change. If you are a business owner and want more time (and fun), read this book.

- **Sharon Jurd, author of How to Grow Your Business Faster than Your Competitor and Extraordinary Women in Franchising**

I've known Michael for over 15 years and worked with him in two of his companies. The material he covers in the Strategic Advisor is absolutely loaded with useful information from his own personal experiences... that any business owner can use to become more successful.

But more than that...

As you'll read in his book, it's one thing to make a lot of money... it's entirely something else to have balance in your personal life, too. And that's what else you'll learn in Michael's book - you'll walk away with tools you can use to win mastery of your emotions, health and relationships, too.

- **Alexi Neocleous, Fubbi.co**

Wow… What a read. An easy and to-the-point book that was fun to read. It has some really great tools and ideas that are not only great for business, but more importantly, the same message could and should be applied to better other lifestyle choices that you will make from time to time.

- **Mark Mahony, Property Investor and Business Owner**

In *The Strategic Advisor*, Michael gives practical advice on how to stay in flow as a business owner and showcases why mindset and health are critical elements to business success. The tools and resources Michael provides in each chapter are easy to access and help you do the 'inner' work so that your 'outer' work has a successful trajectory.

- **Julie Mason, Sales & Marketing Strategist**

This is the most powerful, persuasive and practical book on building a successful business you will ever read. It is full of ideas, wisdom and strategies that will change your thinking forever.

- **Lee Ann Lovegrove, The Happiness Prescription**

This is one of the most refreshing, thoughtful and genuinely informative books on building a successful business I've ever read. The holistic approach is what sets it apart in its field, and it was definitely hard to put it down!

I've known Michael in a business capacity for over seven years and can tell you he lives what he has written on these pages. He is incredibly generous with his time and wisdom and is committed to his passion for sharing his wealth of knowledge with others.

- **Angela Khan, CEO Liquid Project Management**

What a great read! I love the holistic approach in this book. So many profound realisations that explain so much in all areas of my life. Understanding how my beliefs, everyday choices, and past experiences affect my daily progress was a real eye-opener and life-changing.

I now better understand why I am who I am and what I need to do to build a successful business and live my best life. I love the simple action steps at the end of each chapter, and ESPECIALLY all the fantastic golden nuggets shortlisted at the end of the book because just this part alone really makes you think!

Thanks so much, Michael, for this unique gift of knowledge, personal insights, and inspiration. What stands out to me the most is the amount of clarity this book has brought me, personally and professionally. It will, without a doubt, make my life so much easier!

- **Elizabeth Edwards, Owner of Go Nuts Girls**

I found this book very refreshing. It prioritises the person (know and improve yourself) and then deals with the planning and the pennies. It provides terrific advice on effective planning and includes tips I haven't read elsewhere.

- **Professor Craig Pearson FAIAST, GAICD**

THE STRATEGIC ADVISOR

How to Streamline Efficiency and Maximise Profit in Your Business

GLOBAL
PUBLISHING
G R O U P

Global Publishing Group
Australia • New Zealand • Singapore • America • London

DISCLAIMER AND PUBLISHER DETAILS

THE STRATEGIC ADVISOR

How to Streamline Efficiency and Maximise Profit in Your Business

MICHAEL FULLICK

First Edition 2023

National Library of Australia
Cataloguing-in-Publication entry:

The Strategic Advisor: How to Streamline Efficiency and Maximise Profit in Your Business - Michael Fullick

1st ed.
ISBN: 978-1-925370-81-2 (pbk.)

 A catalogue record for this book is available from the National Library of Australia

Published by Global Publishing Group
PO Box 258, Banyo, QLD 4014 Australia
Email admin@globalpublishinggroup.com.au

For further information about orders:
Phone: +61 7 3267 0747

I want to dedicate this book to my Mum and Dad, my brothers, Mark, Jeffrey, and Christopher, to Louise and to my two daughters, Lauren, and Brianna, whom I am very proud of the beautiful girls they have grown up to be. Love to you all.

Michael Fullick

ACKNOWLEDGEMENT

Writing this book was so much harder than I thought it would be but much more rewarding than I could have imagined.

It is the culmination of many years of in-the-trenches experience, research and collaboration with people who have generously shared their time, expertise and support.

This book would not have been possible without the help of this wonderful group of people.

I want to thank the many mentors, colleagues and friends who have supported me over the last 30-plus years, taught me and inspired me to believe I can become the best I can be.

Anthony Robbins, Brian Tracey, Zig Ziglar, Robert Kiyosaki, Jay Abraham, Dan Kennedy, Bill Glazer, Brian Tracey, Ted Nicholas, Tom Hopkins, Scott Hallman, Stephen Covey, Bruce Lipton, Mal Emery and Rich Schefren.

To Mark Mahony, who proved to me, you can actually be in business with someone for a dozen years and still walk away as friends.

To Kawena Gordon, my late 93-year-old life coach, for encouraging me to write this book.

To Scott F, who showed me how to "Fail Fast" by testing ads quickly. You're a legend, Scotty.

To Michael Gerber, thank you for sharing your wisdom and knowledge and teaching me what a successful business should look like.

A Special thank you to Darren Stephens, CEO of Successful Growth Strategies Consulting Agency, for taking the time out of his busy schedule to write the forward to this book.

Also, thank you to Dr Wayne Pickstone, Scott Hallman and David Kolbe for their chapter contributions.

I'm also grateful to my colleagues, friends, and business partners who have shared their insights and feedback, helping me refine and improve this book's content. Their contributions have been instrumental in making this book the best it can be.

Thank you, Ian Marsh, Andrew Carter, Sharon Jurd, Alexi Neocleous, Mark Mahony, Julie Mason, Lee-Ann Lovegrove, Angela Khan, Elizabeth Edwards and Professor Craig Pearson.

To my fantastic team in the office for helping me with graphics and giving me the time to concentrate on writing this book. Ted Marion Hugo, Christian Cañizares, Sydney Alistair Manuel, Mark Chester Damalerio and Ian Jude Colina.

To all the Royal Pines Resort Tees Clubhouse staff where I decided to write the book for their excellent service and friendly smiles, Stephanie, Ted, Andrew, Tiffany, Jemma, Jenny, Nicole, Daniel, Kamelia, Brooke, Oliver, Chloe plus Ben and the other chefs in the kitchen.

Plus, I want to express my sincere thanks to the editors, designers and production team at Global Publishing, who have worked tirelessly to bring this book to life. Their professionalism and expertise have been essential in transforming my ideas into a finished product that I'm very proud to share with readers.

Last but not least, I want to acknowledge the readers of this book, who I hope will find the information and advice contained within these pages helpful and inspiring. This book will help you achieve every personal and business success you desire.

CONTENTS

FOREWORD

Greetings, my friends! It's Darren Stephens, #1 International bestselling author and Entrepreneur, and I am honoured and excited to present to you my friend's latest book, *The Strategic Advisor.* This book results from his lifelong journey of learning and running various national/international businesses and teaching others how to succeed in life & business.

As an entrepreneur, I have spent over three decades studying the strategies and techniques the most successful business leaders have used to create thriving organisations. And in this book, I was amazed at the brilliant concepts and strategies Michael shares, including the secrets he has learned and the tools you can use to transform your business and take it to the next level.

The art and science of building a successful business is not just about having a good product or service. It is about understanding your customers, your market, your competition, and your own strengths and weaknesses. It is about having a clear vision and a strategic plan that will guide you towards your goals.

This book will teach you how to create a strategic plan that is customised to your business, how to identify the right opportunities to pursue, how to build a winning team, and how to create a culture of success. I invite you to join me on this journey and discover the power of *The Strategic Advisor.*

Together, we can unlock your full potential and achieve the success you deserve.

Darren Stephens
#1 International Bestselling Author of
Millionaires & Billionaires Secrets Revealed

INTRODUCTION - THIS BOOK IS DIFFERENT

My Humble Beginnings

I remember when I was about 12, I had a paper run. I got about $10-15 weekly, which was good money then. I liked doing it so much that I did my paper run on Christmas Day. That day, I got the best tips because my customers felt sorry for me. Looking back, my entrepreneurial flair was beginning to show. My business destiny was sealed. But there is more to the story.

Growing up in a small country town, I was getting bored seeing and doing the same thing all the time. I thought, how the hell can I get out of here?

I decided to join the military at the tender age of 17. I remember getting off the bus at the barracks with this man yelling and screaming at us raw recruits.

I thought to myself, what's this guy's problem? What is happening? He must be having a bad hair day. Then, I realised what I had done. And it got worse before it got better! In hindsight, I can see I was there to experience the discipline. Anyone who has served will relate to this.

After my service, I worked for a couple of companies as an employee. As in the military, I didn't particularly like being told what to do, and my heart was tugging me to follow my entrepreneurial flair. So, I began my business journey.

The Art and Science of Building a Successful Business

I wish I had had a book like this when I started my first business over 30 years ago.

This is not your usual "Business How To" book. This book is about producing results for you and your business. If you take action and apply what I will show you, I know this book will change your business, and it will change your life.

In this book, I offer my take on the Art and Science of building a successful business.

There is more to it than just the usual strategies and tactics to build a business. There is a real art to creating a successful business, and it starts with you first and foremost. Then the business second.

Please let me explain…

As important as the business, if not more important, is how your mindset is working to give you the best chances of building a profitable and successful business. It's so easy to have limiting beliefs often taught to you as a child that will sabotage your success.

And often, you will not understand why you are doing it. It just happens on autopilot until you identify and change the limiting beliefs.

This has been one of the hardest things for me to find a solution for. A process that works. And yes, I can prove it works! In 2013 I stumbled across a method that changed everything for me. It was amazing! Worked like clockwork every time.

Using this method in conjunction with muscle testing (Kinesiology), I discovered what my subconscious believed to be true and not true.

For example, I tested the belief statement "I am worthy" to see if my subconscious believed that statement. Well, it turned out my subconscious did not believe "I am worthy". WOW, I thought to myself, what damage is that doing to my personal and business life?

So then, I ran a simple 2–3-minute procedure, and sure enough, after doing another muscle test, I confirmed my subconscious now believed that statement.

Imagine being able to identify your self-limiting beliefs, run a simple 2–3-minute program, and then check the changes that have been made physically.

Why Affirmations Suck in My Opinion

We have all been taught about how beneficial Affirmations are, right? To get them to work, your subconscious must believe the belief statement to make lasting change effectively.

When I work with clients, many will say they have been doing affirmations for years. "Great," I'd say. "Do we mind checking in to see how you're going with that?"

In most cases, all those affirmations they have been doing for years are not anchored into the subconscious. So, it's like saying, "I am worthy" or "I have all the money I need" a million times, and your subconscious is saying, "yeah, sure! I don't believe you!"

As I said at the start, I firmly believe that when we subconsciously make fundamental shifts within ourselves, the sky's the limit.

Use What Feels Right for You.

This book is jammed packed with tools, resources, strategies, and tactics you will find very useful as you adjust your inner world and grow your business. Simple and easy to use and understand.

Please apply what you feel will work for you right now. I am a firm believer in doing what happens with ease. The more you push something or try to force an outcome…you push it further away.

This book is laid out in a very specific way. The book's first half is about you (your inner world), and the second half is about your business (your external world). Also, some of the information is repeated slightly differently in other chapters.

How many books have you started reading and still need to finish because they are too long? This book is to the point and won't take long to read. That's on purpose, so you read the whole book. Please do me the honour of reading to the end. That way, you will get the most value out of this book.

At the end of the book, you will find a resources section that links up each chapter with tools and action steps to take. You can visit the website for additional information where extra resources are being added regularly.

I feel you will enjoy reading and using this book to transform you and your business.

Here's To Creating a Better You.

Michael Fullick

> **"Creating a better you,**
> **Takes courage, focus and follow-through.**
> **But with each step, you'll see it true,**
> **The best version of yourself is in view."**
>
> **- Michael Fullick**

CHAPTER 1

Wealth Conditioning Program for Business Owners

CHAPTER 1

Wealth Conditioning Program for Business Owners

For many years I wondered why I did the things I did in my business and personal life. Consciously I knew what I should be doing but wouldn't do them. I would do enough to survive but not enough to thrive.

Well, I was aware enough that something had to change within me. So I went off and completed a Tony Robbins event in Sydney in the early 90s. It was a great event. There were thousands of people there. The energy in the room was fantastic.

I remember late one night, I was about to "Walk on Fire" and saying the mantra "Cool Moss", thinking to myself geez, I hope this works as I was about to get married in a couple of weeks. Let's say I was walking very quickly when it was my turn! Well, lucky for me, it worked. (There were a few unlucky ones on crutches the next day.)

For the next few weeks, I was on this massive high. I was doing the lymphatic breathing Tony taught me; it really worked to clear my sinuses. Also, I ran one of his processes. And I used this successfully to stop biting my fingernails.

Then I started attending events worldwide, learning from some of the greats of their time. The likes of Anthony Robbins, Brian Tracey, Zig Ziglar, Robert Kiyosaki, Jay Abraham, Dan Kennedy, Bill Glazer, Brian Tracey, Ted Nicholas, Tom Hopkins, Michael Gerber, Stephen Covey, Bruce Lipton and Rich Schefren, to name but a few. For each event, I usually bought one of the programs promoted and got excited that this was the missing link for me to finally be able to move on and be successful in my life.

SUCCESS TIP:

I realised the best information comes from talking to other people at meal times. You get to relax, have a drink, and ask questions. The information I received at the dinners was amazing! As the saying goes, you become like those you associate with!

I was already a very busy entrepreneur and business owner, and many of these programs sat on the shelf, gathering dust, and still needed to be completed. I'm sure some of you can relate to this!

But lucky for me, I completed enough programs so that changes started to happen within me. These subtle changes began to build momentum. You see, I realised I was unintentionally sabotaging my success.

So, I continued learning, attending events and reading as many books as possible, as well as joining the best marketing and business coaching platinum mastermind group at the time in Australia, run by Coach Mal Emery.

Affirmations On Their Own Suck.

Now before you start to get upset with me, please let me explain…

Along the way, I learnt about the power of positive affirmations and began to use them daily. But I wasn't sure if they were working and creating long-lasting changes. Then after a while (well, years later), I realised that affirmations on their own suck…for me, anyway. Why? Because the affirmations I was reciting daily were not turning into reality!

I like this quote from Neale Donald Walsch's Book 1, *Conversations with God*.

"Affirmations do not work if they are merely statements of what you want to be true. Affirmations work only when they are statements of something you already know to be true. The best so-called affirmation is a statement of gratitude and appreciation."

Gratitude and appreciation for what you already have. For example, give gratitude for the car you have right now because it's better than walking. Or your current income (even though it may not be your ideal amount) is better than no income! (More on this in Chapter 4)

Let's continue…

For years I pondered how to prove that a positive affirmation or belief statement is working: that my subconscious accepts the affirmation as being accurate and correct.

Then in 2013, I came across a method that changed everything. Finally, I could physically confirm beforehand that I had a belief that was holding me back from success. I would then make the change in a few minutes, then physically verify that I no longer had this limiting belief affecting me. Wow, I couldn't believe it.

I assure you that this does work and is a permanent change - or until it's no longer required!

But before I get into how this method works, let's talk about your subconscious programming!

Your Subconscious Programming.

I knew deep down at some stage in my life that if I wanted to achieve what I wanted to accomplish in my life, I would have to be prepared to speak in front of others.

The thought of public speaking scared the hell out of me. Seriously. I couldn't think of anything worse. Well, maybe dying was worse!

I couldn't do it. But at the same time, I knew I had to overcome this to achieve my dreams, so how?

My 93-year-old Life Coach at the time said I would be running live events soon! I was not one to argue with her; she could get pretty feisty, you know. I knew she was right.

But how was I going to remove this fear of public speaking?

A good friend, Ian Marsh from Streetsmart Marketing, said he knew someone called Darren who could help.

So I built up the courage and red-eyed a flight to Melbourne, Australia, to see this guy whom Ian recommended.

I was sitting in the room feeling extremely uncomfortable as he sat with me, explaining his approach and asking me questions; I didn't know if his process could help me.

"Michael, tell me about what happened when you were a young boy."

"Um…where do I start," I thought to myself as it was a vague question, and then it just came to me.

When I was a young boy, I remember I used to get into a lot of trouble. Not bad trouble with the law or anything like that. My brothers and I were adventurous and just having fun. But my dad didn't see it that way. It felt like every weekend I was getting into trouble for something. Mum would say, "Wait until your father gets home." I would cringe, waiting for the second he walked in the door. He'd line up the three of us. He would say, "Ok, what have you done now? Who is responsible?" Usually, I was the main perpetrator and copped the discipline first. It was not pleasant, to say the least.

After a while, I realised the best thing to do was deny everything, keep my head down, and say nothing until I had to.

I don't blame my dad; he was doing what he was taught to do by his family.

Anyway, what Darren came up with was that because my subconscious had been conditioned to keep my head down and say nothing, that was sabotaging my ability to speak in front of others.

He did his magic and set some new beliefs for me during the session.

And it worked like magic. Before I knew it, I was running live events called the Happiness Club and felt very comfortable speaking in front of others.

Around this same time, my dad was very unwell with cancer. We had been travelling back and forth from clinics in Australia and Malaysia to help give him the best chance of survival.

Unfortunately, in 2018, my dad passed, and I had the honour of giving his obituary in front of the congregation. If I hadn't overcome my fear of public speaking, I would never have been able to do that. I am sure it would have become one of my life regrets.

My point is that we are all subconsciously conditioned by those closest to us during our very influential childhood years.

I like to use the analogy of a brand-new filing cabinet.

Imagine all the drawers in the filing cabinet are open and empty. When you hear affirmative or limiting beliefs, they get filed away as folders in your filing cabinet. The files continue to fill up until around the age of seven.

Then the drawers in the filing cabinet close, and you run these beliefs as programs for the rest of your life. This becomes your reality. And you will likely pass these programs on to your children unless you take action to change them. Because this is what you believe to be true. It's not your fault. It's just how your mind works.

Have you ever heard the statement, "You're becoming just like your mum or dad?" Well, there is a reason for that! You're running the programming they have taught you as a child. As you get older, you become just like them.

Did you know that from a young child to about seven, you are in a trance state, also known as a hypnotic state? What this means is that whatever you have heard or seen is taken as being true without question.

For example, if you ever heard "Money doesn't grow on trees", "you will never amount to anything", or "you're not worthy", well, that gets locked into your subconscious as being 100% completely true.

The Wealth Conditioning Program for Business Owners

Let me introduce my secret weapon, *The Wealth Conditioning Program for Business Owners.* My team and I have successfully used this program to help transform hundreds of clients' personal and business lives.

This method uses a specific program along with muscle testing or kinesiology that taps into your subconscious to make the changes. Using this method, you can ask yourself, for example, "I am worthy", and with physical muscle testing, you get an answer. You will get a yes/no answer.

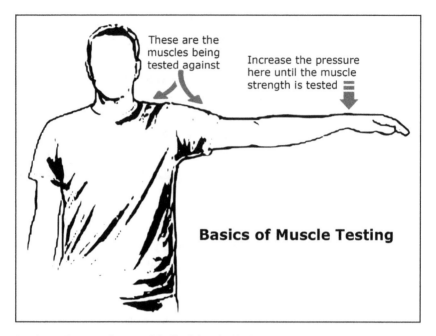

These are the muscles being tested against

Increase the pressure here until the muscle strength is tested

Basics of Muscle Testing

So, how do you change this limiting belief once you get a yes/no answer?

Here is the overview of the Program.

The Wealth Conditioning Program for Business Owners aims to clarify your beliefs and how they affect your business and personal life. By clarifying the beliefs statements in this program, results are usually felt immediately and will continue to unfold after each session.

Also, during each session, you will create Action Steps of easy and doable things you can do now. This helps to manifest your new beliefs. You then continue with your action steps until you achieve the results you want. Results like improvements in your business success, relationships, self-love, abundance, money, purpose, confidence, health, well-being, intuition and many more.

As I have said, your beliefs are locked into your subconscious mind by around the age of seven, and as adults, you use these beliefs (those of a seven-year-old) to navigate life and, at times, wonder what you are doing wrong when success isn't flowing easily to you.

Many of your beliefs have been picked up from family members and authority figures.
Beliefs like "money doesn't grow on trees" or "you have to work hard for money" can limit the abundance and prosperity you are willing to receive.

Once we identify which beliefs no longer serve you, we upgrade your belief system just as you would upgrade your mobile phone with the latest software version.

How do we 'upgrade' your belief system?

We use specialised 'balances' that allow your brain to sync with both hemispheres of the brain, creating the perfect opportunity to release what is no longer serving you and receive the beliefs you want to embrace.

These balances are easy, painless, efficient, and highly effective. Once the balances are complete, your subconscious mind is filled with affirming belief statements that it will use to help you create the level of success you dream of.

The program is completed over three sessions, a week apart, via three zoom calls. We can work with you regardless of your location anywhere in the world.

The Program covers six critical areas of your personal and business life.

1. Business / Career
2. Money / Wealth
3. Relationships
4. Happiness
5. Health and Wellbeing
6. Procrastination / Decision making

Here is the Initial Questionnaire we ask clients to complete before we proceed to upgrade their belief system. Along with the belief statements, we check and make changes accordingly.

Go ahead and see how you would rate yourself for the following questions. This will give you a baseline to show you where improvement is required.

The Wealth Conditioning Questionnaire for Business Owners

How would you rate the following statements on a scale of 1-10? 10 = amazing and 1 = not very good.

Business / Career

1. I own a successful and profitable business.
2. I love the business I'm in.
3. I feel good about going to my business/work.
4. I am open to new business possibilities.
5. I worry and stress about my business.

	1	2	3	4	5	6	7	8	9	10
Q1										
Q2										
Q3										
Q4										
Q5										

Belief Statements

1. I am worthy of my successful business.
2. I am worthy, and I deserve all the world has to offer me.
3. My business is an expression of my creativity.
4. I am successful in my business.
5. My business is filled with joy, laughter and abundance.
6. Everything I touch is a success.
7. I turn every experience into an opportunity.
8. New doors of opportunities are opening all the time.
9. I move forward in life to my next opportunity.
10. I am open to new business possibilities.
11. I collaborate with successful people.

Money / Wealth

How would you rate the following statements on a scale of 1-10?
10 = amazing and 1 = not very good.

1. I have enough money to pay my expenses.
2. I am in a good financial position.
3. My income is increasing every year.
4. I am open to new business possibilities.
5. I give myself permission to be successful.

	1	2	3	4	5	6	7	8	9	10
Q1										
Q2										
Q3										
Q4										
Q5										

Belief Statements

1. I am worthy of money, abundance, and prosperity.
2. My income is constantly increasing.
3. I prosper wherever I turn.
4. I am a magnet for money and opportunity.
5. Money comes to me in unexpected ways.
6. Money comes to me in new and exciting ways.
7. I give myself permission to prosper.
8. I embrace my full financial potential.
9. I love having financial freedom.
10. I live in an abundant world, and I have access to an unlimited supply.

Relationships

How would you rate the following statements on a scale of 1-10?
10 = amazing and 1 = not very good.

1. I associate with successful people.
2. My personal relationships are good.
3. My business relationships are good.
4. I am lonely in my business.
5. I am good at building relationships.

	1	2	3	4	5	6	7	8	9	10
Q1										
Q2										
Q3										
Q4										
Q5										

Belief Statements

1. I release past relationship hurts.
2. I have trust in all of my relationships.
3. I give love to others with ease.
4. I am loving, lovable and loved.
5. I am worthy of love.
6. I attract wonderful, loving relationships into my life.
7. I am safe in all of my relationships.
8. My relationships are fulfilling on all levels.
9. I am grateful for the learnings in my relationships.
10. I easily communicate openly in my relationships.

Happiness

How would you rate the following statements on a scale of 1-10? 10 = amazing and 1 = not very good.

1. I love and accept myself.
2. I am happy and content with my business.
3. I am happy and content with my life.
4. I smile a lot.
5. I put myself first.

	1	2	3	4	5	6	7	8	9	10
Q1										
Q2										
Q3										
Q4										
Q5										

Belief Statements

1. I am entitled to experience the joys of life.
2. I allow happiness to shine through.
3. I express my happiness with ease.
4. I express my joy with ease.
5. I am open to receive joy & happiness.
6. I deeply love and accept myself.
7. I feel happier and happier each day.
8. I am happy and content in my life.
9. I am happy and content with my business.
10. Every cell in my Being is full of happiness and joy.

Health and Wellbeing

How would you rate the following statements on a scale of 1-10?
10 = amazing and 1 = not very good.

1. I exercise regularly.
2. My diet is healthy.
3. I get plenty of sleep.
4. I love my life.
5. I drink at least 2 litres of water per day.

	1	2	3	4	5	6	7	8	9	10
Q1										
Q2										
Q3										
Q4										
Q5										

Belief Statements

1. I live a vibrant and healthy life.
2. I radiate optimal health.
3. Every cell in my body is happy and healthy.
4. I digest life with joy and ease.
5. I am healthy, whole & filled with joy.
6. I maintain my body at optimal health.
7. I am filled with life, energy and the joy of living.
8. I easily release what I no longer need.
9. Every day in every way, I am growing healthier and healthier.
10. I open myself to the wisdom within.

Procrastination / Decision Making

How would you rate the following statements on a scale of 1-10?
10 = amazing and 1 = not very good.

1. Making decisions is easy for me.
2. I often make the right decisions enabling my goals to be achieved.
3. I procrastinate in my business.
4. I follow what feels right when making decisions.
5. I feel I am in tune with my wisdom and knowledge.

	1	2	3	4	5	6	7	8	9	10
Q1										
Q2										
Q3										
Q4										
Q5										

Belief Statements

1. I release my procrastination and increase my motivation.
2. I release my procrastination and allow clarity & change.
3. I release all procrastination and stagnation.
4. I release all procrastination blocking my willpower and motivation.
5. I make clear decisions free from procrastination.
6. I have the confidence to make decisions.
7. Making decisions is easy for me.
8. My decisions are always aligned with my highest good.
9. I make the right decisions enabling my goals to be achieved.
10. I am free from distractions when making decisions.

I'm sure you will agree that completing this initial questionnaire will give you insight into areas of your life that may be subconsciously sabotaging your success. And where improvements can be made.

By registering for *The Wealth Conditioning Program for Business Owners,* you will have a way, with our help to upgrade your belief system and confirm that your subconscious mind has accepted the changes.

Are you ready to take yourself and your business to the next level?

Action Steps:

1. Complete *The Wealth Conditioning Questionnaire for Business Owners.*

2. Register for your FREE 20 min assessment to see how you can register for the Wealth Conditioning Program for Business Owners by visiting:

   www.TheStrategicAdvisor.com.au or email

   support@TheStrategicAdvisor.com

Resources:

Go to www.TheStrategicAdvisor.com.au/resources and download all the links for this chapter.

Or use your phone to scan the following QR Code:

Plus, all the links are included in the Resources Section at the end of this book.

> **"Your business is nothing more than a distinct reflection of who you are. So, if your business is to change – as it must continue to thrive – you must change yourself first. If you are unwilling to change, your business will never be capable of giving you what you want."**
>
> *-Michael Gerber*

CHAPTER 2

What You are Naturally Good at When You Take Action

CHAPTER 2

What You are Naturally Good at When You Take Action

As I mentioned in the introduction, I had a paper run as a teenager—delivering newspapers to people around town. It felt good to provide a service to others and get paid at the same time.

From then on, I knew I wanted to be of service to others and own my own business. But there was more to this than I realised.

In my early years in business, I had to do everything myself—bookkeeping, sales, marketing and providing products and services to my customers. I thought this was a regular part of owning and operating a business. How wrong I was!

I suffered from an "Entrepreneurial Seizure". I was good enough technically to do the work but could have done better at owning and operating a business. (More about that in Chapter 6).

I got thrown into the deep end, so to say!

But when you think about it, isn't this what happens to most people who want to start their own business?

You start with good intentions to make more money and get more freedom and time.

But you don't realise what it takes to own and operate a successful business.

And especially, you do not want to fail at being in business.

One day a good friend of mine, whom I can honestly say, dollar for dollar, is the best marketer I have ever known, said something I have never forgotten…

> **"Michael, if I can give you one word of advice… Fail fast! The quicker you find what does not work, the closer you will get to finding out what does work"**
>
> **- Scott F.**

So, it's best to find out what you are good at and try to do that as much as possible, as quickly as possible.

There was just me. As I mentioned, I had to do everything in my first business. After a while, I realised I was good at about 20% of everything that had to be done.

I had to keep learning and doing more training to get better. But honestly, I still sucked. I beat myself up about this for many years.

Then one day in 2011, I came across a fantastic tool called the Kolbe A™ Index.

Kolbe A™ Index.

This Index changed everything for me… an "aha" moment for me, if you will.

The index took about 20 minutes, and I received a comprehensive report.

After reading the report in detail, I was blown away.

Wow, I thought this all made sense now. For years I'd been beating myself up about procrastinating all the time, but now I find out I'm very good at doing things at the last minute. I permitted myself to be me. To be my authentic me. That's just how I am wired! Such a relief that this was a game-changer for me.

The biggest takeaway from this assessment was that as a 7 in Quick Start Mode, I am very good at doing things at the last minute. Plus, the report advised me to Race the clock, Take on Challenges, Promote alternatives and Experiment.

What is the Kolbe A™ Index?

The Kolbe A™ Index (Instinct Test) is unique. It does not measure intelligence, personality or social style. It measures the instinctive ways you take action when you strive. Use your custom results to be more productive, less stressed, and unlock joy at work with your family.

Kolbe measures your instinctive way of doing things, and the result is called your MO (method of operation). It is the only validated assessment that measures a person's conative strengths. Unlike any other evaluations or quizzes you've taken, Kolbe gets directly at how you execute (not your IQ or personality).

SUCCESS TIP:

This tool helps you identify what you're naturally good at when you take action, regardless of your age or education level.

Why should you take the 36-question Kolbe A™ Index?

- You'll learn to focus your time and energy to be more productive and achieve your goals.

- The 4 Number Kolbe A results will direct you towards more effective communication, career choices and study habits.
- Relationships with loved ones and co-workers will start to feel more natural because you'll learn to trust your instincts instead of trying to change each other.

Once you have your Kolbe A™ Index, watch the video (Link in the resources section) on how to apply it to your life and improve your productivity.

Over 1 million people have used the KOLBE Index to understand their natural strengths.

Here are my results as an example for you:

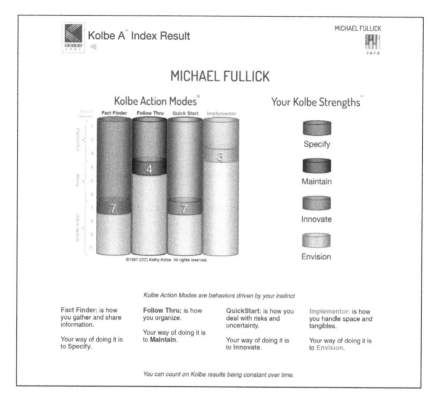

Now, what will you do about your results once you have your results?

How about you work towards only doing what you are naturally good at? Work to your strengths, not your weaknesses. Of course, it may take some time to outsource your other tasks, but at least now you have somewhere to start. You now know how you are wired.

SUCCESS TIP:

Do what you are good at and outsource the rest.

Hiring Staff and Using Outsourcing in Your Business.

As the business owner, you have the most significant responsibility of all!

Make your business successful while not burning out or giving up during the process.

I've often heard the saying that the business owner eventually runs out of time and money, but I'd like to add that they also run out of enthusiasm. One day you wake up and say, "I've had enough."

And in my experience building and selling businesses for 30-odd years, I realised that the sooner you can get others to do the work you don't want to do (or are good at), the better you will feel in your business. The more your business will be worth when you go to sell it. The better your business will operate.

How does The Kolbe System™ help me grow and optimise my business?

Of course, you would also use this fantastic tool when hiring staff. So, you find the perfect fit for a job role.

The Kolbe System™ helps you achieve what you care about the most.

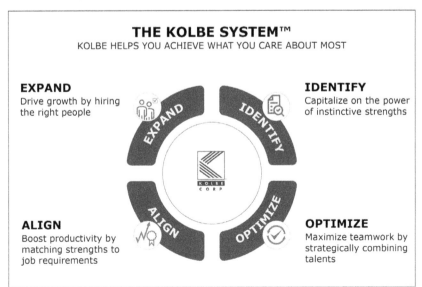

THE KOLBE SYSTEM™
KOLBE HELPS YOU ACHIEVE WHAT YOU CARE ABOUT MOST

EXPAND
Drive growth by hiring the right people

IDENTIFY
Capitalize on the power of instinctive strengths

ALIGN
Boost productivity by matching strengths to job requirements

OPTIMIZE
Maximize teamwork by strategically combining talents

- Expand – Grow your Business by hiring the best people
- Align – Boost your Productivity, matching strengths to job requirements
- Identify – Capitalize on the power of your instinctive strengths
- Optimise – Strategically combine your talents to maximise teamwork

One of the things Kolbe talks about is more than just hiring someone who is likeable and has the qualifications and skills to do the work. But someone who can naturally solve problems or take action in a role that aligns with how they are wired. How they NATURALLY take action.

This will also help you to retain more staff over the long-term.

This tool will help you find staff who are an excellent fit for your business.

Also, you can interview someone who is not quite a fit for the role you have in mind. But are more suitable for another position in your business.

What's your time Worth as the CEO and Business owner?

What's your time worth? $50, $100, $200, $500, even $1000 an hour? Even at $50 an hour, there are stacks of tasks you shouldn't be doing.

Let's look at this in more detail.

It's essential to understand the actual value of your time. This will help you realise you will be much better off working on your business than in it.

Most of us start a business hoping to achieve a flexible schedule, a good salary and even sell the company in the future.

However, what often happens is that you get caught up in the business's day-to-day operations by juggling multiple roles, including managing staff, business development, and cash flow, while even trying to do the actual work—no wonder you are crazy busy all the time.

To achieve your desired outcomes, you must stop working in your business and start working on it, and the key to this is understanding the value of your time as the CEO and business owner.

By prioritising tasks and delegating responsibilities, you can create a more sustainable and successful business that will lead to greater financial success.

Now I'm starting to feel some pushback from you.

If you are a two-person business, you will be doing much more operational work than a more established company with five to ten staff. But my point here is that regardless of your business size, please consider what can be given to others.

For example, if you are doing a role that usually pays $30 an hour, that's what you are getting paid then. The more you do, your income will be limited to that level.

The trick is to work out your current hourly rate and consider ways to increase it to your desired level.

Here's the formula:

Your Hourly rate = yearly salary (plus allowances) + Business net profit
The Actual Yearly Hours You Work

For example: $100,000 Salary + $30,000 net profit
1920 hours (40 hrs/wk for 48 wks)

$130,000/1920 = $67 per hour.

The next step is determining how many hours you work on those activities that usually pay the lower hourly rates.

Let's say you can identify 3 hrs a day and get someone else to do the lower-paying work or outsource it remotely. That 15hrs a week x 48 wks = 720 hrs a year.

What lower-paying activities should you get others to do as quickly as possible?

- Any receptionist work, including answering the phone
- Office Administration
- Bookkeeping or accounts
- Customer Service
- Lower-level sales and marketing activities
- Product research and development
- Taking and managing orders
- Receiving and dispatch activities
- Doing the actual work in your business

What higher paying or value add activities could you do with that extra time?

Activities that add value and have the highest profit-making potential for your business.

Things like…

- Building customer relationships
- Building your team
- New marketing and sales strategies and tactics
- Reviewing your monthly financials every 30 days and
- Continue building systems to automate your business
- Continue to innovate to stay ahead of your competition
- Use the S-Curve to watch your business growth and opportunities
- Take time out to THINK

Of course, this depends on your business model, but a lot can be delegated or outsourced remotely.

So now you will be working on your business, not in your business, and your income and business profits will increase accordingly.

> **SUCCESS TIP:**
>
> Answer the phone within three rings. Why? Amazing how much business can be lost because you didn't answer the phone quickly.

Outsourcing in Your Business

It continues to surprise me how much talent is available for hire. I mean brilliant and talented people who want to work casually—project to project.

They work remotely from home, so they don't have to commute. I also feel the new generation coming through is more than ever wanting to create a work-life balance right from the start of their careers.

But some will work for you full-time if you know where to look.

What's the Process for Outsourcing?

1. Decide on what you want to outsource
2. Is it a part-time or full-time position
3. Have a list of systemised duties and timeframes for completion
4. Advertise, hire, and train the right Virtual Assistant (VA)
5. Track and measure their performance

How does it all work for me?

Years ago, when I started outsourcing, I used Upwork and, more recently, Fiverr. Suitable for the project to project activities. But after a while, I wanted full-time staff working for me.

Why? Because good VAs are always busy. I didn't want to keep training new VAs all the time.

The best place I found to hire staff was in the Philippines.

The Philippines is a very popular location for hiring full or part-time staff. Many big companies like Amazon, Verizon, Microsoft, HP, Accenture, Expedia, JP Morgan etc., have teams there. The Philippines is 2hrs behind Australia, so the time difference works.

Some companies in the Philippines offer what's called a seat lease. This means you rent a desk with a chair and computer, fast internet, staff amenities, etc., for a fraction of the cost of hiring local full-time staff in your home country. Here's how it works...

You can be up and running for a monthly seat lease of USD 200 and pay the staff member $5-10 USD per hour. Plus, many of the staff available are already trained and ready to go depending on the required skill set. Many are university qualified and speak excellent English.

After researching, I decided to use a seat lease company called Delonix based in Cebu. They had great staff but no real loyalty to me because they were contracted to me but worked for Delonix. That's fine; just the way that model works.

SUCCESS TIP:

It's important that your remote staff work from an office, NOT from home.

Now I will give you a tip... wherever possible, your remote staff needs to be in an office and NOT work from home. The Philippines is notorious for flooding, losing power, poor internet connection or the internet going down altogether.

I can help you here… I have an office in Cebu that can offer a seat lease service to you.

My staff will advertise locally and help you hire the right team (for a fee) based on your requirements.

They will get them set up in the office. And then you take over and get them up to speed with your business.

Our modern office has two high-speed internet connections, air conditioning, a backup generator, and staff amenities and is in a flood-free zone close to the city. See the resources section for more information.

By the way, answering your phone can be easily handled remotely. Yes, that's right, the person answering the phone does not have to be physically in your office.

Action Steps:

- Complete your Kolbe A™ Index and download the report. **https://www.kolbe.com/the-kolbe-system/**

Or use your phone to scan the following QR Code:

Resources:

Go to www.TheStrategicaAvisor.com.au/resources and download all the links for this chapter.

Or use your phone to scan the following QR Code:

Plus, all the links are included in the Resources Section at the end of this book.

> **"Michael's strategies have proven to help business owners leverage The Kolbe System™ for their own and their business success."**
>
> **- David Kolbe**

The Kolbe A™ Index, The Kolbe System™ and Kolbe RightFit™ are the trademarks of Kolbe Corp or Kathy Kolbe. All rights reserved.

CHAPTER 3

*The Power of Knowing
Your Numbers*

CHAPTER 3

The Power of Knowing Your Numbers

I'm sure you've heard the expression, "go with the flow". Here is a mathematical way to learn what that means to help you better understand when and when not to do things in certain areas of your business and personal life.

Have you heard of Numerology? If you are familiar with Astrology, you may know a bit about Numerology. They are both similar in some ways. Simply speaking, numerology is the study of the numbers in your life. Knowing your numerology numbers can help you better understand yourself and the flow of life.

This chapter is based on Pythagorean Numerology. This "Science of Numbers" is called Numerology. Numerology has existed for centuries, dating back to Pythagoras, born in 608 BC. He founded his university in southern Italy around 532 BC.

Numerology is based on your birth date. It allows you to extract information and knowledge about your inner self. Once you understand that information, you can create a more fulfilling and purpose-driven life.

In a way, it is a heads-up about how you are wired. Also, it helps to show you what opportunities and challenges you may face during your life.

Now there is a whole heap of information you can get using numerology, but for this chapter, I will focus on your birth path/life path number and personal year numbers. To keep it simple. And then show you how you can use this personally and in your business. I will add some links in the resources section if you want to know more and how these fit into the 9-year cycle we are all on.

How to Calculate your Life Path/ Birth Number

Let's say you were born on 6/6/1965. You break it down this way…

6+6+1+9+6+5= 33

Then you break the 33 down to a single digit.

3+3 = 6

So, in this example, the life path number is 6.

If you want to check your Life Path number online, here is a handy tool:

https://www.peacefulwarrior.com/life-purpose-calculator/

Or use your phone to scan the following QR Code:

What your Life Path Number Means

Using Pythagorean numerology, there is no Life Path Number 1. Some other systems do use a Life Path Number 1. However, In Pythagorean numerology, Life Path Number 10 is used instead of Life Path Number 1.

Life Path #2

Life path #2 represents a person who is cooperative, empathetic, and sensitive to the needs of others. If this is your number, you are naturally diplomatic and have a strong sense of empathy, making you more effective at mediating and resolving conflicts. You are also highly intuitive and have solid emotional intelligence, allowing you to connect with others deeply.

Life Path #3

Life path #3 represents a creative, expressive, and sociable person. If this is your number, you have a natural talent for communication and self-expression and enjoy being the centre of attention. You are optimistic, energetic, and highly imaginative, which helps you to approach life with a positive and playful attitude.

Life Path #4

Life path #4 represents a practical, organised, and hard-working person. If this is your number, you are often known for your strong work ethic and attention to detail, which makes you efficient and reliable. You value stability and security and are often drawn to careers in fields that offer a sense of structure and routine. You are also logical and methodical in your approach to life and have a strong sense of responsibility.

Life Path #5

Life path #5 represents an adventurous, spontaneous, and versatile person. If this is your number, you have a natural desire for freedom and a thirst for new experiences, making you well-suited for careers that allow for travel, creativity, and independence. You are also known for being adaptable because you can easily handle change and uncertainty. You are often highly communicative and enjoy meeting new people and learning from different cultures.

Life Path #6

Life path #6 represents a nurturing, responsible, and compassionate person. If this is your number, you strongly desire to help others and often find yourself drawn to health care, education, or social work careers. You also value stability and balance in your personal and professional lives and are known for your strong sense of responsibility and dependability. You are naturally caring, responsible, and often looked up to as community leaders.

Life Path #7

Life path #7 represents a person who is introspective, intuitive, and spiritual. If this is your number, you are often an independent thinker and enjoy delving into your thoughts and beliefs. You have a strong sense of intuition and are often highly perceptive, allowing you to see what others may miss. You may be drawn to careers in spirituality, philosophy, or the arts and are often described as spiritual seekers.

Life Path #8

Life path #8 represents an ambitious, driven, and successful person. If this is your number, you are often drawn to careers in business, finance, or law and have a strong drive to succeed and attain material wealth in success. You are confident, assertive, and often seen as a leader in your field. You are also highly organised and efficient and can effectively manage your resources to achieve your goals.

Life Path #9

Life path #9 represents a compassionate, selfless, and idealistic person. If this is your number, you are often drawn to careers in humanitarian work, the arts, or spirituality and strongly desire to impact the world positively. You are highly empathetic and compassionate and often put the needs of others before your own. You may also be known for your strong sense of justice, fairness, idealism, and wisdom for a better future.

Life Path #10

Life part #10 is considered to be a master number. If this is your number, you are often highly ambitious and visionary, with a strong desire to succeed and positively impact the world. The number 10 also represents a turning point or a moment of transformation, indicating that you embark on a journey of personal growth and spiritual evolution with this life path number.

Life Path #11

Life path #11 is also considered to be a master number. If this is your number, you are often highly intuitive, visionary, and spiritual, with a strong desire to use your gifts to serve others and positively impact the world. You have a natural sense of inspiration and are often seen as spiritual leaders and teachers. The number 11 also represents a spiritual awakening and enlightenment path, indicating that you are on a journey to develop your intuition and spiritual gifts.

Life path #22/4

Life path #22/4 is also considered to be a master number. If this is your number, you are often highly practical, visionary, and ambitious, with a strong desire to positively impact the world. You can turn their big ideas into concrete, realistic plans and are often successful in your personal and professional lives. You are also known for your strong sense of responsibility, stability, and dependability.

How to Calculate Your Current Personal Year in the 9-Year cycle?

It's easy to calculate your personal year number. Use your day and month of birth, but replace that with the current calendar year instead of your birth year.

Using the example above, you were born on 6/6/1965. Instead of using your birth year, replace that with the current calendar year of 2023.

You break it down this way…

6+6+2+0+2+3= 19

Then you break the 19 down to a single digit.

1+9 = 10 = 1+0 = 1

So, in this example, the Personal Year number is 1.

If you want to check your Personal Year number online, here is a handy tool:

https://www.peacefulwarrior.com/life-purpose-calculator/

**Or use your
phone to scan the
following QR Code:**

What is the 9-year Cycle, and how can I use it?

According to numerology, we all go through a rhythmic cycle that lasts nine years. So, if you are 45 years old, you have completed five cycles. 5x9=45. Each cycle builds on the previous cycles.

You can probably remember times in your life when you had significant progress and other times things seemed to drag on and annoy you.

By understanding where you are in the 9-year cycle, you can learn to go with the flow as your 9-year cycle unfolds. For example, if you are in a one year, that's a time for new beginnings, in an 8-year time to reap what you have sown. In a nine year, it's a time for completion preparing for the new.

As you travel through your nine-year cycle, I believe this energy is reflected in your business as you are also the business owner steering the ship. This has been my personal experience.

Between each personal year, there is a changeover period of a few months.

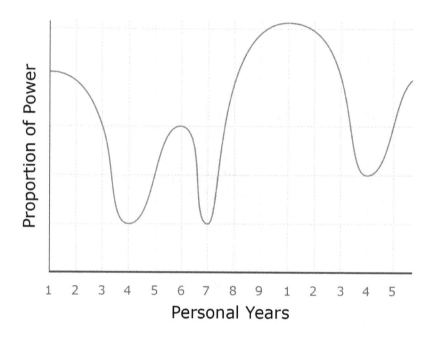

Year 1 - New Beginnings

A year of new opportunities and possibilities. You are taking risks, starting new projects, taking on new responsibilities and setting new outcomes. An excellent time for personal growth as you are being asked to dare to be different.

A time to take action, learn new skills and make things happen, like launching new products, entering new markets or expanding your business.

Personally, a great year to move house or sell your business and other assets like investments or real estate.

Year 2 - Balance and Building Relationships

A year for building relationships, working with others, and finding balance in your business. A time to focus on being sensitive and understanding to others. This could mean investing in staff development and engagement and building strong partnerships with suppliers and important stakeholders.

A time to focus on financial stability and security in your business and reputation. This could include implementing systems in your business, such as setting budgets and forecasts.

With this year's energy, you may have an increased sense of intuition that could encourage you to find space and time to sit quietly and reflect. AKA meditation!

Year 3 - Innovate and Building Reputations

A year to express creativity and innovation by finding new ways to communicate with your customers. Also, you may develop new marketing strategies, launch new services or products and find new ways to reach and engage customers.

A time to focus on building a solid reputation and positive image. This may include developing a strong brand and message, plus making an excellent online presence.

Take action to see what happens. You may conceive and discuss new ideas and anything that feels right. However, handling vulnerability and doubts may arise. "Am I good enough to do this" You will be fine. Just go with the flow.

Year 4 - Building a Solid Foundation

A year to focus on building a solid foundation by improving your systems and procedures due to the evolution of your business over the last few years. With a focus on efficiency and practicality. This can lead to long-term success and good growth in your business.

Stability is also required to regroup and consolidate from previous years' growth.

We are looking for anything overlooked, so we are well positioned for the new opportunities that will present next year.

Personally, a time to rest and relax. Remove what is no longer required, even take a holiday.

Like a Y7, this is a time of stabilisation, not expansion. A year to consolidate and not make any significant changes in your business.

Year 5 – Creating New Opportunities

A year that is associated with change, freedom and diversity. A time to be adapting to and embrace new opportunities and be open to different perspectives. It is being open to new ideas, new ways of doing things and working with new technologies.

Also, an opportunity for your business to diversify in terms of your workforce and customer base. This way, you can find ways to serve a more diverse customer base.

It is a time to focus on the freedom to innovate and be creative, including the freedom to make changes and take risks.

Year 6 – Sharing, Harmony, and Balance

This year is associated with you taking on greater responsibilities and finding balance in your business. A good year for you to focus on harmony and balance in the workplace with you and your staff.

Also, you could focus on finding ways to give back to your community by supporting charitable causes by donating some of your time or money.

Personally, it is a time for you to find positive work-life balance and focus on the home and personal relationships. At this time, relationships are either enhanced or released.

Year 7 - Learning and Reflection

A time for gratitude for how far you have come. A time for you to step back and evaluate the overall direction of your business and focus on the long-term goals and the bigger picture.

A good time to focus on what you have learnt using your wisdom and knowledge gained so far. A time to invest in training programs for you and your staff as well as R and D to stay ahead of your competitors.

Like a Y4, this is a time of stabilisation, not expansion. A year to consolidate and not make any significant changes in your business.

A time to reflect on the previous year's experiences and the wisdom that comes with personal experience. Also, no significant changes are advised in your home affairs.

Year 8 - Financial Success

If you have taken action and done the work required, this year is a year to reap the rewards of your efforts over the past seven years. This could also mean expanding your business through profitable mergers, acquisitions, or strategic partnerships to increase revenue and profits.

This can be a year of rapid change as we emerge from the previous year of consolidation. New opportunities may arise, but be wary of the shiny objects that may distract you.

A good time to establish your business as a leader in your industry by investing in branding and marketing to help achieve your long-term growth outcomes.

This an excellent time to be more conscious of your business' impact on the world and how you can align your business values for the good of one and all.

Personally, a great time to expect more money and abundance in your life.

Year 9 – Completions and Closure

The number 9 is associated with completion, closure, and endings. This a great time in the 9-year cycle to prepare your business for sale. A good time to finish projects or bring closure to certain parts of your business. Also, an excellent time to reflect on the business's journey. Evaluate what has and hasn't worked and learn the lessons that have been presented.

Also, an excellent time to let go of the past and prepare for a new phase in growth and development.
Personally, a time of travel, making new friendships and ending relationships that no longer serve you. This helps to make way for the new energy coming through in a one year.

As I said earlier, there is so much information on this subject. I will add more details in the resources section at the end of the book and on the website.

Action Step:

- Work out your Life Path number and Personal Year number by visiting: **https://www.peacefulwarrior.com/life-purpose-calculator/**

Or use your phone to scan the following QR Code: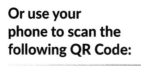

Resources:

Go to www.TheStrategicAvisor.com.au/resources and download all the links for this chapter.

Or use your phone to scan the following QR Code:

Plus, all the links are included in the Resources Section at the end of this book.

> ## Get out of your own way and go with the flow and the energy of life.
>
> ## - Michael Fullick

CHAPTER 4

Money, Success, and Happiness in Your Business

CHAPTER 4

Money, Success and Happiness in Your Business

Why money and a successful business don't necessarily buy you happiness - it may do the opposite.

Congratulations, you've got a pretty good business! So why are you still not 100% happy, working more hours than you want to, and thinking about your business all the time? Well, please let me explain.

While financial success in your business may bring temporary satisfaction, it may not equate to long-term happiness. Here are some factors that may contribute to this.

1. **Hedonic Adaption**: We all tend to quickly become accustomed to new possessions and experiences, causing the initial joy to fade away.

2. **Materialism:** An excessive focus on money and material goods can lead to feelings of emptiness and dissatisfaction, as they do not meet your deeper emotional and spiritual needs.

3. **Stress:** Operating a successful business can be stressful and detrimental to your mental and physical health.

4. **Relationships:** Business success can sometimes lead to neglecting meaningful relationships such as family and friends, which are crucial for happiness.

5. **Purpose:** Having a sense of purpose is essential for happiness, but business success or wealth may not provide that sense of purpose.

Don't get me wrong, I'd rather have a great business making good money than not, but at what price? What I'm saying is that it's all about finding the balance.

Please think about this as soon as possible.

That means asking yourself how much money is enough.

What will you do and won't you do for money?

How big do you want your business to be? How many employees, how many sales, and how much profit?

I say this from personal experience. The second business I owned had so many staff that my business partner and I ended up running the company to pay for the staff and overheads.

The work-life balance! We would have been much better off halving (or more) the operation and taking more money ourselves instead of feeding it back into the business. But we didn't set the time and money balance we wanted to achieve.

And, of course, you don't get back the time. And as you get older, time often becomes more important than money.

In my experience, you will have 10% of your employees do not show up for work on any one day. So, if you have 50 staff, you have five away. If you have five staff, maybe one doesn't show up. Which one of these would create the least amount of stress?

I found a good balance of 5 employees to one business owner gave the right money life balance. Of course, this will depend on your business model.

Therefore, finding that balance, having a sense of purpose and nurturing relationships are essential to achieve overall happiness and well-being.

Oh, come to think about it, my current business has five employees! Well, there you go!

Happiness

You can experience happiness in many forms. Like the feeling of reaching a specific outcome. The contentment of being around your family and friends. Or the pleasure of experiencing something new and exciting.

For some of us, happiness may be found simply by reading a book or spending time outdoors. For others, the sense of joy may be tied to experiences of success and achievement.

Something to remember is that happiness is not a constant state. In life, as you know, we experience ups and downs. This means you get the opportunity to experience duality.

This means you get to experience what feels right to you and what feels wrong to you. What feels happy and what feels sad to you? If you haven't experienced unhappiness, how can you know when you are happy? Money, no money. Love/hate etc.

This opportunity to experience duality helps us to remember who we really are!

A great way to become happier is to practice gratitude.

Being happy and giving gratitude for what you already have

Being happy and giving gratitude for what you already have are closely related. Showing gratitude involves recognising and appreciating the good things in your life rather than focusing on what is lacking.

For example, if you ask for more time, the fact you are asking means you are coming from a place of lack!

If you focus on lack, you will get more lack. That's how it works!

Gratitude is integral to the law of abundance because it helps you focus on what you already have instead of what you lack. You can see the good already in your life when you are grateful. This positive mindset helps attract more abundance because you focus on the positive rather than the negative.

Giving gratitude with a positive mindset can help improve how you are feeling and your overall well-being.

Research suggests that practising gratitude can lead to increased happiness and reduced symptoms of depression and anxiety. It can also help to improve your relationships, as it promotes feelings of connection and positivity towards others.

Some ways to practice gratitude include:

- You keep a journal and write down things you are grateful for daily
- You are sharing your gratitude with others by donating to a worthy cause
- You reflect on the good things in your life before going to sleep
- BE in the present moment instead of dwelling on the past or worrying about the future. When you focus and operate in the present moment, you will find it easier to appreciate what you already have instead of constantly striving for more

Please don't underestimate how important it is to keep a journal. I remember one day having a cuppa with my then 93-year-old life coach. She told me, "Michael, one of my biggest life regrets was not keeping a journal. When you get to my age, you forget a lot!"

> ## SUCCESS TIP:
>
> The Law of Detachment states that true success comes from being detached from the outcome and focusing on the present moment.

Your Life Purpose

In my opinion, your purpose in life is to remember who you really are! To uncover the infinite potential that lies within you. To discover your unique qualities and talents and use them to impact the world positively.

Remembering who you really are is a lifelong journey of self-discovery, self-acceptance, and self-love.

As you begin to remember who you really are, you will start to see that you are not just a physical body but something much more. You will begin to understand that you are not separate from the world around you but an integral part of it. You will start to recognise that you are not just a consumer but a creator. You'll see you can shape your reality and manifest your wishes and desires.

As you remember who you really are, you will start to see that your past, present or future do not limit your true self. You will understand that your thoughts, emotions, or experiences do not restrict you. You will begin to recognise that your fears, doubts, or insecurities do not limit you.

Remembering who you are is about finding your place in the world and your home in the universe. It's not just about discovering your purpose but your inner drive. It is not just about finding your calling but your destiny.

It is not just about finding your path but finding your way home. Your purpose in life is to remember who you really are, and in doing so, you will discover the truth of who you are and the truth of the world around you.

SUCCESS TIP:

Your purpose in life is to remember who you really are.

While you are pondering that…

Begin With the End in Mind.

Let's begin with the end in mind. Think of it this way… What would you like people to say about you when you are gone? How you lived your life. Your achievements. Your family. Your friends. What legacy do you wish to leave behind? Etc.

Then work backwards!

What do you wish your life to look like? Actively create your life on a day-by-day basis!

Where do you want to be in 1, 5yrs, 10, 20, or 50 years?

If what you want the most is a lot of money to give away best, you have a vehicle/ business to get you there. And be doing it.

When is enough, enough? A bigger house, more money, a flashier car etc.?

Remember, you can't load everything into a U-Haul trailer and take it with you!

Here are a couple of strategies you can try.

Future Pacing Strategy.

Imagine what your future looks like in vivid detail, how it feels, looks, and sounds. Imagine five years in the future, and you are writing a one-page letter about what that future looks like for you in a perfect and ideal world.

What house you live in, what car your drive, what relationships you have, how much money you have, what work you are doing, whom you are helping, etc. What you have achieved and the dreams that have come true.

By doing this exercise, you tap into your subconscious mind, which helps to influence your thoughts, emotions and behaviours positively. Reviewing this letter often will help you anchor a strong connection between your conscious and subconscious mind that will improve your motivation and focus on creating this future outcome.

Obituary Strategy.

What would you like others to say about you at your obituary? The strategy involves writing your obituary as if you have lived a long and fulfilling life.

The idea behind this strategy is that by considering what you want your legacy to be, you can gain greater clarity and focus on what truly matters to you in your life.

So once again, write a one-page letter about what your achievements, relationships and contributions have been to others. Also, include how you want to be remembered and your impact on the world.

Then Review this letter often and work towards creating this reality.

SUCCESS TIP:

The Law of Giving - the more you give away, the more you get back.

Why Putting Yourself First is So Important

A late good friend of mine and life coach (she was 93) said to me one day…

"Michael, you know it's very important to put yourself first. Because if you don't, how can you expect to be able to be of service to others? Michael, please remember you are not being selfish but being self-aware". I have never forgotten this!

When you first start applying this habit, it can be challenging, mainly if you are used to putting the needs of others before your own.

When you put yourself first, you take responsibility for your happiness and well-being rather than relying on others to fulfil this need. This can help with your self-esteem as well as improve your relationships.

What's important to note here is that this does not mean being selfish or disregarding the needs of others, just about finding balance and being considerate of others' needs. But while also making sure your own needs are met.

So please allow making time for yourself in mind, body and spirit. Life is about being, not doing. BE in the present moment, BE who you really are, BE your authentic you. And then DO what matches that!

For example… You're taking a shower. Rather than thinking about what's on your to-do list for the day, why not just BE and enjoy the shower? BE in the present moment.

> ## SUCCESS TIP:
> **Don't fight the Flow...Be the Flow.**

Plus, at some stage in your life, you will begin to ask yourself what you will and won't do for money! And Time!

Dr Wayne Pickstone talks about in Chapter 5 how those with money who are sick would gladly give up their money to be healthy again. Often a bit late, then. Difficult to rewind the clock.

How to Put Yourself First

Putting yourself first is an essential aspect of self-care and your personal growth. Here are some tips on how to do it.

1. **Identify your priorities**
   Take some time to think about what's most important in your life. This could be your business outcomes, your relationships, or something else. Once you know your priorities, you can start focusing on them

2. **Set clear boundaries**
   It's essential to set limits on what you are willing to tolerate in your relationships and interactions with others. This will help you protect your time and energy for the things that matter most.

3. **Learn to say no**
   This was a tough one for me. I'd say yes, all the time, and it just got me into trouble.

Saying no to things that don't align with your priorities can be difficult, but it's necessary so you can put yourself first. Practise saying no politely and assertively, and remember that it's OK to say no to the things that don't serve you.

4. Take care of your physical and mental well-being
Putting yourself first means taking care of your physical and mental health. This includes getting enough sleep, eating well, exercising and engaging in activities that bring joy and relaxation.

5. Make time for yourself
It's essential to make time for yourself, even if it's just a few minutes a day. This might mean reading a book, going for a walk, or simply sitting in silence.

6. Invest in yourself
Investing in yourself means taking the time and effort to improve yourself, learning new skills, taking courses or developing new hobbies and practising self-compassion. Being kind and compassionate to yourself is a crucial aspect of putting yourself first.

7. Practice self-compassion
By speaking to yourself with kindness and being gentle and understanding when you make mistakes.

8. Learn to recognise and challenge negative thoughts
Recognising negative thoughts or self-talk that might be holding you back is essential. For example, you may think, "I don't deserve to take time out for myself" remind yourself that you are worthy and deserving. (see Chapter 1)

9. Learn to let go
You may be holding onto things that no longer serve you. It could be a toxic relationship, either a personal or a business relationship. Or you may be having a grudge. Time to let go of these things. Because at some stage, you will realise life is too short to be bothered with these things.

10. Surround yourself with positive people
The people you surround yourself with can significantly impact your attitude. Make an effort to surround yourself with positive, supporting people who will lift you up and encourage you for yourself first.

The Power of Sitting Quietly and Breathing

I'm the first to admit I resisted doing this for a very long time because I had no time! Well, I have come to realise that this is even more important than doing ANY work in my business. It prepares me for my day—an opportunity to centre my thoughts and focus.

Please give yourself permission daily to sit quietly and concentrate on your breathing. Slow deep breaths and sit upright in a comfortable chair. Now, this is where I get some pushback. What do you mean by sitting quietly and doing nothing? I have so much work to do, no time to waste.

Right. Well, couldn't you give yourself the gift of just 15 minutes each day to relax and focus on your breathing? I'm not talking about 30 mins or an hour but 15 minutes.

Yes, this is also called Meditation.

One of my favourites is a guided meditation where I listen to a 15-minute recording by Ester Hicks called *Getting into the Vortex*. She talks you through the process and helps regulate your breathing. In the end, you feel so good. I will add some links in the resources section.

The Silva Method

I have known about the *Silva method* for quite some time. It builds on basic meditation methods, and it's surprising how quickly and easily you can learn how to relax and control your mind. If you want to take your meditation to the next level, check out this program.

The *Silva Mind Control method* is a pioneering program that empowers you to transform your life through meditation and visualisation.

Initially released in 1978, the book and audio program has assisted millions of people in over 100 countries worldwide in enhancing their lives and achieving greater happiness and success.

Drawing upon the innovative course developed by Joe Silva in the 1960s, this comprehensive yet user-friendly program shows you how meditation and visualisation can harness your mind's full potential and unlock its immense power.

Some of the Benefits of Using the *Silva Mind Control Method*

- Improved Concentration and Focus: This method teaches you how to enter a state of deep concentration, known as the alpha state, to improve your focus and attention.

- Increased Creativity and Intuition: The program emphasises the importance of assessing the right side of your brain, which is associated with intuition, creativity, and imagination.

- Better Problem-Solving Skills: The Silva Method provides techniques for accessing your inner wisdom and intuition to solve problems more effectively.

- Enhance Memory and Learning: The program includes exercises that can help you improve your memory and learning abilities, such as visualising information to make it easier for you to remember.

- Stress Reduction and Relaxation: The Silva method teaches you how to enter the alpha state, reduce stress and increase feelings of relaxation.

- Improved Relationships: The program includes exercises designed to help individuals improve communication and relationships with others.

- Increased Self-Confidence and Self-Esteem: By practicing these techniques in achieving your goals or outcomes, you can experience increased self-confidence and self-esteem.

Interesting fact: According to the book _Altered Traits_, 44% of American Fortune 100 companies offer meditation training to their employees.

Action Steps:

- Download and listen to Abraham Hick's Meditations every day https://www.amazon.com.au/Getting-Into-Vortex-Meditations-Download/dp/1401962114

- Download and listen to The Silva Method https://www.amazon.com.au/Silva-Mind-Control-Method-Revolutionary/dp/B09PFCJPYP

Resources:

Go to www.TheStrategicAdvisor.com.au/resources and download all the links for this chapter.

Or use your phone to scan the following QR Code:

Plus, all the links are included in the Resources Section at the end of this book.

> **"The two most important days in your life are the day you are born, and the day you find out why!"**
>
> **- Unknown.**

CHAPTER 5

Some Straight Talk About Your Health and Well-Being as a Business Owner

CHAPTER 5

Some Straight Talk About Your Health and Well-Being as a Business Owner

I have been a student of health and well-being for as long as I can remember—a good habit from my military days. You just had to be fit and healthy to do that job. This has carried on over the years. Looking back, I'm glad It did.

I started a supplements business years ago, selling our products to a targeted market.

And still today, I own a health and fitness business selling products worldwide.

You meet people you resonate with and form good long-term relationships along the way.

Dr Wayne Pickstone (Dr of Chinese Medicine) is one of those people. A genuine and caring person. Highly qualified with many years of experience helping thousands of clients, including myself.

Wayne recommends you implement a holistic, well-rounded health plan that includes what you eat, how you exercise and what he calls his "One Weird Technique". More on that later.

But first, let's talk about exercise. You've heard all the reasons why exercise is essential for your body. But I'd like to introduce you to what Wayne recommends.

Exercise

With exercise, here's the best and simplest Wayne has come across and has been doing for years.

It's important to ensure you are following the three concepts while you are doing the exercises.

1. Shoulders Back
   • Shoulders back and shoulder blades move toward the spine
   • Try and keep them here during each exercise

2. Tighten the core
   • Squeeze the muscles that would stop you from urinating and defecating while at the same time tighten the abdominal muscles below your navel

3. With each exertive part of the exercise, breathe out

These exercises help to increase nitric oxide and exercise over 180 muscles.

Links to examples of exercises can be found in the resources section. These anaerobic or calisthenic exercises revolve around helping the body use Nitric Oxide for muscle growth. Nitric Oxide is made by the body that feeds your muscles and allows them to grow.

No weights or heavy lifting is required. You can do the exercises anywhere; the more often you do them, the better your results. Plus, these exercises take just minutes to do. So, no excuses for not having enough time.

Diet

Wayne recommends an alkaline Mediterranean-style diet that includes these servings per day:

   • 3 to 5 serves of protein
   • Six serves of vegetable
   • 2 to 4 serves fruit
   • 2 Serves of nuts, seeds and oils
   • One small serving of grains (Optional)

- One small serving of dairy (Optional)
- 2 Litres of water per day
- Use Liberally fresh herbs, spices, garlic, lemon, lime juice, and honey

An example meal plan and list of foods PDF can be found in the resources section on the website.

My One Weird Technique

Wayne has developed what he calls his "One Weird Technique" in his clinic that's so powerful that he has clients who are Medical doctors, Functional Medicine Practitioners, Chiropractors, Naturopaths, Physiotherapists, Health Advocates and Business owners.

Wayne has kindly agreed for me to share his unique technique with you.

This is going to be a different discussion on health and well-being.

Wayne will give you much relevant and valuable information in this chapter. By the time you get to the end of this chapter, you will understand the following:

Why from an Ancient Medicine perspective, there is only one cause of all diseases and challenges in life. ONLY 1.

There may be many drivers and triggers, but there is only 1 CAUSE.

More about that shortly . . .

As you read through the following chapter, look for the words "drivers" or "triggers" to see what Wayne means.

In life, there are typically three things you aspire to . . .

1. To have great relationships with your partner, your children and immediate family and friends.
2. To have financial freedom where you're not relying on government handouts, pensions etc.
3. To have excellent health.

I'm sure you'll agree.

Having numbers 1 and 2 from the above list is difficult, sometimes impossible or cannot be achieved if your health has been challenged.

For example, Wayne has spoken to many millionaires, and they will gladly give away their wealth to get their health back. It's nice that they can afford it.

He has also spoken to tens of thousands of people who are not as financially well off, but they say the same thing; they will do whatever is possible, including selling their most valuable assets to get their health back.

Did you know there is a health epidemic that is totally out of proportion to what most people think is occurring today?

To demonstrate this, here are some facts:

- All chronic conditions are on the rise. Did you know 1 in 2 People in the Western World now suffer from chronic diseases like Cardiovascular Disease, Diabetes, Cancer and Dementia?

- Diabetes is becoming the biggest epidemic of the twenty-first century.

- 1 in 5 of all ages have chronic pain.

- 1 in 10 has Arthritis.

- More people than ever suffer from depression – around 264 million people.

- 63% of people over 18 are now overweight or obese.

- Sperm counts have decreased by 50%.

- Our governments don't know where to put their Alzheimer's and chronic disease patients.

- Statistically, by the time you reach the age of 40, you will have six hidden diseases.

Let's repeat the last statistic so you can wrap your head around it.

Statistically, by the time you reach the age of 40, you will have six hidden diseases.

If you are 40 or over and have great health, excellent.

However, the above statistics show that some hidden diseases may lurk, which is worth exploring.

Usually, it takes the next 10 to 20 years (30+ if you're lucky) for these hidden diseases to manifest. Men are the most affected, and at this point, you may not believe this . . . walk into any aged care facility, and its residents will most likely be 80% women and 20% males.

Unfortunately, the males died earlier.

One of Wayne's favourite sayings. . .

When someone says to him, "I feel great" (especially males), his response is always:

"That's great, but please allow your blood tests to prove you are healthy."

Now the challenge is reading your blood results correctly because, surprisingly, the reference ranges we are given in our lab results are for really sick people.

There's a smaller range for healthy people that should NOT be exceeded.

Now let's look at some business stats.

According to the U.S. Small Business Administration, over 50% of small businesses fail in the first year, and 95% fail within the first five years.

. . . and according to the London and Zurich bank, the Five Common Causes of Business Failures are:

- Poor cash flow management
- Losing control of finances
- Bad planning and a lack of strategy
- Weak leadership
- Over-dependence on a few big customers

and another statistic that is becoming more widely known:

- Half of the world's net wealth belongs to the top 1%
- The top 10% of adults hold 85%
- While the bottom 90% has the remaining 15% of the world's total wealth

Why is this so?

What if poor health, business, financial failure, or lack of financial resources are linked?

Let's find out together . . .

These statistics are shocking; they can even be horrifying. If we want to change them, the question is, 'Are we up to the challenge?'

Right now, you may be thinking, 'How could this even be done?' and it's an excellent question.

Let's look at how . . .

From an Ancient Medicine perspective, there are 3 Steps to getting well and 3 Steps to getting sick. Luckily, they are the same 3 Steps but in reverse order.

Collectively, this 3-Step Process is what Wayne calls "my **One Weird Technique**".

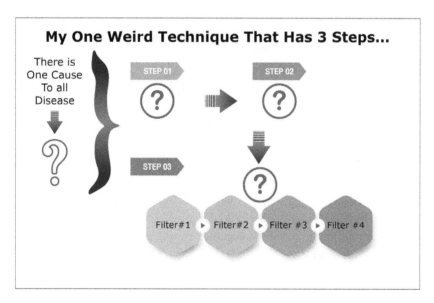

Step #2 Represents your Symptoms or the analogy of a Fire

Let's start at Step #2 in the above diagram, where Step 2 represents your symptoms.

Your symptoms are specific to you, and everyone's symptoms are different.

Let's use an analogy to help you understand.

The analogy is that of a fire.

Think of a real fire, and that fire starts at Step #2 of the 3-Step Process.

From an Ancient Medicine perspective, fire represents cold, dampness, wind, heat and fire.

Ancient Medicine has always said you can heal nearly all diseases by changing our behaviour and environment. Western Medicine aligned with this way of thinking in the last few decades when they coined Epigenetics. These are the words from Traditional Chinese Medicine that reveal to us how the environment impacts our health.

Epigenetics is the study of how your behaviour and environment can cause changes that affect the way your genes work. It's interesting how Ancient Medicine has known this for 4,000-plus years, but Western Medicine has only just accepted this concept.

One of the biggest challenges with Western Medicine is that it's only as good as the technology of the day.

The technology of the day in the 1850s said that doctors didn't have to wash their hands between delivering babies.

In the 1940s, the technology or science of the day said it was okay to spray people with DDT pesticides.

In the 1950s, the day's technology said smoking reduces stress, and it was okay for pregnant mothers to smoke. There are many, many more examples we could use.

Western Medicine is brilliant in crisis care.

If you have a serious car accident or need a heart valve replaced or a liver transplant, Western Medicine undoubtedly has the answers. However, with disease management, as the statistics above suggest, we need to look deeper.

Now let's get back to Ancient Medicine themes . . .

Cold entering your body can affect circulation, brain fog and thinking speed.
If wind enters, it can cause muscle twitching in different parts of your body, like wind moving through the trees. For example, wind can manifest as fibromyalgia because the pain migrates from muscle to muscle.
Now for this chapter, let's use the word "fire" to describe all of the above elements (cold, damp, wind, heat and fire) to make it easier to understand.

A fire can be mild, moderate, severe or catastrophic. As mentioned earlier, fire represents our symptoms in the human body, and your symptoms can be mild, moderate, severe or life-threatening.

From an Ancient Medicine perspective, we use the word fire; however, from a Western Medicine perspective, the words used are chronic inflammation and oxidative stress.

The combination of chronic inflammation and oxidative stress are the primary drivers of all diseases and the major drivers as to why you do not achieve your six, seven or eight-figure goals in your business.

In other words, why you may fail.

More about this shortly.

When the fire (or the chronic inflammation and oxidative stress) takes over, the following are symptoms that you may experience . . .

Suppose mild to moderate oxidative stress is present. In that case, your symptoms can be cold hands and feet, joint pain, brain fog, lack of clarity, difficulty making decisions, poor circulation, excess weight, feeling lightheaded and shaky, craving sweets and pins and needles or nerve pain.

If severe oxidative stress has taken over, please see the left-hand side of the following health scales diagram.

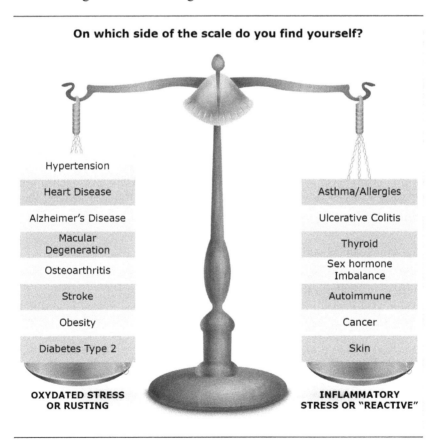

On which side of the scale do you find yourself?

Hypertension	
Heart Disease	Asthma/Allergies
Alzheimer's Disease	Ulcerative Colitis
Macular Degeneration	Thyroid
Osteoarthritis	Sex hormone Imbalance
Stroke	Autoimmune
Obesity	Cancer
Diabetes Type 2	Skin

| **OXYDATED STRESS OR RUSTING** | **INFLAMMATORY STRESS OR "REACTIVE"** |

If life-threatening, it's a heart attack or stroke.

Suppose mild to moderate chronic inflammation takes over. In that case, symptoms manifest in the sinus, hay fever, bloating, heartburn, reflux, moodiness, skin challenges, irritability, anxiety, emotional ups and downs, irrational decision-making, and lack of libido.

If severe chronic inflammation has taken over, please see the right-hand side of the health scales diagram.

If life-threatening, it's cancer.

And yes, you can have both. For example, you can have mild to moderate oxidative stress where you might have joint pain, brain fog, and light headedness with chronic inflammation symptoms of bloating, heartburn, itchy skin, and irritability.

Hopefully, you can see how your health can directly affect your ability to make the right decisions in your company as a business owner.

Step #3 Here comes the fireman to put out the fire.

The 3rd step using the "fire" analogy could be likened to how the Fire Brigade assesses how they manage the fire. After the assessment, they can determine how best to fight the fire.

The same can be said for the human body.

Step #3 is all about the 4 Firemen or the four filters.

The 4 Firemen are in order;

- Filter #1 - the digestive system
- Filter #2 - the liver
- Filter #3 - the immune system and
- Filter #4 - the kidneys

Each has its associated symptoms, and protective firewalls should not be breached between the four firemen (or 4 Filters).

Let's look together at each and reveal how they can affect you, both from a physical point of view and an emotional point of view. . .

Filter #1 = The Digestive System

Physical Symptoms:

- Bloating, wind, Constipation, Diarrhea, Reflux, Heartburn, IBS, leaky gut, sinus, hay fever, postnasal drip, Mucous.

Emotional Symptoms:

- Worry, low self-esteem, obsession, easily crying, defensive, compelled to neatness.

As mentioned before, there is a "firewall" between each filter, protecting it from the following filter being affected. However, if the "fire" or oxidative stress and chronic inflammation penetrates the firewall, the fire moves into the liver and drives the following challenges.

Filter #2 = The Liver

Physical Symptoms:

- Blood sugar challenges to diabetes, overweight, gritty, sore eyes, floaters in the eyes, visual challenges, tired but gets through the day, thyroid challenges, unable to detoxify, iron or iron storage challenges including B12 and folate, and gynaecological challenges.

Emotional Symptoms:

- Irritability, Anxiety, depression, anger, resentment, stubbornness, headaches, poor sleep, muscle aches and pains, cramps, and involuntary muscle movements.

If the "fire" or oxidative stress and chronic inflammation penetrates the next firewall, the fire moves into the Immune System and drives the following challenges.

Filter #3 = The Immune System

Physical Symptoms:

- Obvious symptoms like heaps of colds, flu or autoimmune

- Cryptic symptoms like no colds or flu, especially for three years or more

Emotional Symptoms:

- Shame, embarrassment, awkwardness, confusion, easily bullied

If the "fire" or oxidative stress and chronic inflammation penetrates the next firewall, the fire moves into the kidneys and drives the following challenges.

Filter #4 = The Kidneys

Physical Symptoms:

- Bone or joint pain, Obesity / serious weight challenges, hearing challenges,
  UTI / bladder or kidney infections

Emotional Symptoms:

- Panic attacks, OCD, PTSD, fear, paralysed, timid, impending doom, dread, chronic fatigue, can't get out of bed, memory challenges

Lastly, there should be a firewall protecting any breach past the kidneys. However, suppose the fire, oxidative stress, and chronic inflammation penetrate the kidneys. In that case, you may be facing life-threatening challenges like cancer, stroke, or a heart attack can manifest.

For you, the business owner, please look at the different emotions that now come into play when each one of these 4 Filters and how they may affect you.

You can see how this can make a huge difference in your decision-making process.

Now there is a caveat here. You may not know you have a problem.

You may have gone to your doctor, who said your bloods are normal. Do you know why? Because the reference ranges for reading serious diseases are very wide.

I'm sure you've heard of the fit person who goes for his daily run and dies of a heart attack. Now that is not normal.

Typically, early warning signs show up in the body as:

- Filter #1 compromised, gut symptoms - low self-esteem and you may worry a lot - maybe some bloating with constipation.

- If the firewall is breached, Filter #2 is compromised, and the fire moves into the liver – then some irritability and anxiety – with some headaches, you may feel tired, muscle cramps and sleep challenges.

- If the firewall is breached again, Filter #3 is compromised. The fire moves into the Immune system – confusion sets in, and it becomes challenging to make decisions – and you notice you catching everything of late or even more concerning if you have NOT had a cold or flu for longer than three years – this means your immune system is so compromised you can't catch a cold of flu.

- If the last firewall is breached, Filter #4 is compromised. The fire moves into the kidneys – some panic attacks are noticed, and you feel more paralysed/stuck in your life/business - more brain fog, forgetfulness occurs, extra weight piles on and more joint pain, lower back pain etc.

Therefore, if you came to see Wayne and said you have lower back pain (kidney compromised) with no other symptoms, he would immediately know that the kidney filter (Filter #4) is affected. Then he works backwards (From Filter #4 back to Filter #1).

He'd also know that the immune, liver, and digestive systems are compromised, and chronic inflammation or oxidative stress is raging through your body.

Overwhelm is a common theme. You may feel stuck in your business, paralysed, and find it difficult to move forward. (If you can relate to these emotions and have no physical symptoms, you now know why. It would be a good idea to get your bloods checked ASAP.)

Hopefully, you can now see how your health immediately affects how you run your business or find financial freedom.

It's no wonder the instructive statistics are that 95% of businesses fail within the first five years, and half of the world's net wealth belongs to the top 1%.

To become a healthy business owner, you must break this cycle.

Step #1 Explained

Right now, you may be thinking, 'What is step #1'? it's a good question because it is the most important.

Let's go back to the analogy of the fire.

What two things are going to make a fire get out of control?

Just ponder on that question for a sec.

Two things determine the intensity of the fire. One is dryness, and the second is windspeed.

However, if a fire starts without any wind, after an eight-year drought or where there have been recent rains, where everything is nice and green, or in a rainforest, mother nature will just put out the fire quickly.

However, if a 160km or 100 miles per hour wind drives a fire, no one can put out this fire.

Even if thousands of emergency workers, firefighters and helicopters drop water bombs, this fire is so intense that no one can put it out.

Visualise this picture of the fire is out of control because of the wind speed. The faster the wind, the more catastrophic the damage, especially if it gets up to 160 km or 100 mph.

If we bring this analogy back into the human body, Step #1 is about understanding pH and alkalinity strength.

If the pH gets below 5.8 of urine or saliva and the strength of alkalinity gets below 40, this is the equivalent of a 160 km or 100 mph windspeed.

No one can put out this fire.

Therefore, step #1 represents wind speed and being alkaline.

Practically, if you have any challenges, whether with finances, health or relationships, pH and strength of alkalinity are the drivers.

You can treat with antioxidants, and anti-inflammatories, take on a healing-the-leaky gut program, liver, immune system or kidney detoxification programs. Still, if your body is acidic, you won't see the desired results.

Also, when you're acidic, here's a small list of what else can happen.

Up to 80% of oxygen can't be used.

- When we breathe, oxygen maintains life. But when acidic, the oxygen you breathe now feeds oxidative stress and chronic inflammation (the Fire), sometimes by up to 80%. Think of blowing on fire compared to using a fan.

- The stronger the breeze, the hotter and more ignited the fire becomes. The more acidic you are, the more the oxygen you breathe feeds oxidative stress and chronic inflammation (the Fire).

Up to 50% of food can't be digested.

- Food, unfortunately (even organic healthy food choices), now ferments in your body. If you ferment anything for long enough, it will create alcohol, which could then make possible liver challenges.

Redox Signalling Molecules decline at a faster rate when acidic.

- Your first question might be . . . 'What are Redox Molecules, where are they made, and what do they do?'

- They are communication molecules in your body; without them, it's like having a mobile phone without a sim card.
- They tell all cells how to heal by talking to your genes – epigenetically.
- They activate the immune system to destroy diseased cells. Any antioxidant can't work without Redox molecules.
- They moderate stem cells.

The mitochondria make Redox molecules out of salt water. Did you know that you are, on average, 70% water but more importantly, you are approximately 70% salt water?

How do Redox Molecules decline?

- You lose approximately 10% per decade from the age of puberty.
- When you're acidic, you lose Redox molecules faster.
- Stress, EMFs, chemicals, toxins, and processed Foods also decrease Redox molecules.

There are about 50 trillion cells in your body, and typically when you reach 50, around 40% or 15 trillion cells don't know how to heal until Redox molecules are supplemented.

Redox molecules were only discovered in 1998, which is why you may not have heard of them.

Dehydration

- Some are aware, but most are NOT aware they are dehydrated. The more cracks present on your bottom lip, the more possible dehydration is prevalent. Key electrolytes that prevent dehydration are Bicarbonate, Magnesium, Sodium, Potassium, Chloride, Phosphate, and Calcium.

You can only detoxify appropriately if you have adequate amounts of sodium and/or potassium.

Free Calcium

- This one can be nasty. When dehydration occurs, or we lose our electrolytes, magnesium, phosphate and potassium decrease, and our body becomes acidic. Then your body looks for calcium and takes it out of your fingernails, teeth, and bones because it can't find enough calcium in your food.

  Now it becomes unbound, free calcium, like slithers of glass moving through your arteries, causing chronic inflammation and oxidative stress.

  Your free calcium risk index (FCRI) can be measured. If it's above 0.8, it can create some nasty illnesses:

  0.8 to 1.5 = lack of flexibility, varicose and spider veins, cold hands and feet, heart risk factors begin – blood pressure.

  1.5 to 2.2 = calcification = osteoarthritis / osteoporosis.

  2.2 and above = Cancer, ocular degeneration, cataracts, severe degeneration.

Cells Lock

- When acidic, your cells become locked. Your acidic cells do this by creating a protein that surrounds the cell. The more acidic you are, the more cells lock, making it more difficult to heal. Your immune system is now unable to see that these cells are nasty.

Hopefully, you can now see how vital step #1 is within the 3 Step process.

Blood Chemistries Explained

Let's talk more about blood chemistry.

The process of advanced Blood Chemistry/Pathology testing is a significant step as these extensive test results reveal just what is happening in your body – the same tests your doctor ordered.

However, Wayne's interpretation is different.

Even though the same numbers are being looked at, the interpretation is the compelling difference.

We look at Optimal Ranges that are different from the Normal Reference Ranges . . .

For example… (These do vary depending on the Pathology Lab)

- The Normal Reference Range for Glucose is between 3.33 to 6.38;
- The Normal Reference Range for Thyroid or TSH is between 0.35 to 4;
- The Normal Reference Range for Insulin is between 0 to 25.

Whereas…

- The Optimal Reference Range for Glucose is between 4.05 to 4.9;
- The Optimal Reference Range for Thyroid or TSH is between 0.8 to 2.3;
- The Optimal Reference Range for Insulin is between 3 to 5.

Firstly, have an in-depth look at the gigantic difference between the two.

If your Blood Chemistry results were…
- Glucose = 6
- Thyroid or TSH = 3.7
- Insulin = 12

Glucose's highest optimal range is 4.9, and the above example of 6 for glucose is significantly higher.

TSH or your primary thyroid marker's highest optimal range is 2.3, and the above example of 3.7 for TSH is also significantly higher.

These results suggest possible blood sugar challenges with glucose at six and insulin at 12, as well as low thyroid activity that is sub-clinical and a body that is struggling to get well.

However, from a Western Medicine perspective, you would have been told that you are healthy or that your results were normal.

From the above information, when looking at Step #3 (the 4 Filters), we know that blood sugar and thyroid are related to the liver.

Here's the last piece of the puzzle, as promised:

> ## SUCCESS TIP:
>
> **There is only One Cause for All Diseases, All Disharmony, All Financial Challenges, and All Relationship Hardship, and it is known as The Mistake of the Intellect.**

In other words, the way you interpret stress.

So, the One Cause of all Diseases is the Way you Interpret and Manage Stress.

Your stress is different from your friend's stress. You might enjoy heights and public speaking, whereas your friend would rather die than jump out of a plane or speak publicly.

These are subconscious beliefs that run your daily life.

If negative subconscious beliefs are common, negative things happen in your life.

If positive subconscious beliefs are your natural thoughts, positive outcomes occur.

However, Western Medicine says it differently.

They say, "up to 95% of who we are was pre-programmed before the age of seven." Once again, this level of thinking from Western Medicine has only evolved in the last 20+ years, whereas Ancient Medicine has known this for some 4000+ years.

I also prefer Ancient Medicine's description, suggesting it's a mistake, meaning it can be remedied. In contrast, Western Medicine's description suggests it is programmed, meaning it's more complicated or nearly impossible to fix.

Therefore, if your thoughts are predominantly negative (a mistake of the intellect), they can be changed to more positive subconscious beliefs. How do you know if your thoughts are predominantly negative?

All you have to do is look at how your life is travelling in the three areas that were mentioned above.

1. Do you have great relationships with your partner, your children and immediate family and friends?
2. Do you have financial freedom where you're not relying on government handouts, pensions etc? and thirdly.
3. Do you have excellent health?

If relationships are going well, then your thoughts are predominantly positive.

If your business, your wealth creation and passive income are not going so well, then your thoughts are predominantly negative.

And if your health is not going so well, then your thoughts in this area are predominantly negative.

For most we don't like to think that our subconscious thoughts can be so far out of tune, but if we have an open mind, and we understand what has just been said, these subconscious thoughts can be easily changed.

I've taught meditation, mediated with 5,000 to 10,000 people, been to different parts of the world seeking answers, been a hypnotherapist, taught various Kinesiology techniques, completed Reiki degrees, completed master classes in mind-body medicine, and used frequency machines.

I have found that the method Michael discusses in Chapter 1 is the best way to help you remove subconscious beliefs.

Heartfelt Mediation is also a significant part of my daily routine.

Now you have the complete package.

Now you know, there's ONLY one cause to all disease, all disharmony, and there are 3 Steps to getting well and unlocking your wealth and freedom goals. . . .

To become the On Purpose Business Owner.

Step #1- Alkalise your body

Step #2 – Decrease Chronic Inflammation and Oxidative Stress

Step #3 – Detox the four filters

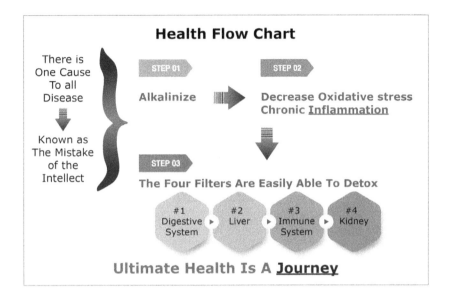

Action Steps:

- To get your free digital downloads and webinar, please go to

  https://OnPurposeEntrepreneur.com

  Or use your phone to scan the following QR Code:

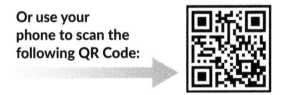

- If you wish to contact Dr Wayne Pickstone directly, please send an email to support@onpurposeentrepreneur.com

Resources:

Go to www.TheStrategicAdvisor.com.au/resources and download all the links for this chapter.

Or use your phone to scan the following QR Code:

Plus, all the links are included in the Resources Section at the end of this book.

> **"**
>
> *"For the on-purpose entrepreneur to have an aligned business with abundant profits, momentum, continuous growth and a positive ethos, the physical body must be in optimal health and well-being because limited subconscious beliefs are otherwise difficult to change."*
>
> *- Dr Wayne Pickstone*

CHAPTER 6

Let's Talk About Your Business

CHAPTER 6

Let's Talk About Your Business

During my 30-plus years in business, building and selling businesses, plus working with other business owners, it's amazed me how many of these businesses did not know their crucial business metrics and how to get them. I'd say it was like three in 100 knew their numbers. And to be honest, in my early days in business, I didn't know my numbers or how to find them.

In this chapter, I will cover some basic business metrics and simple things you can do to make your business life much easier. And expand on as your business grows.

But before we dive into that, can I ask you a few questions?

What business are you in?

Or should you be in business at all?

Yes, this may be a bit confronting.

But please let me explain…

What Business Are you really in?

When I ask this question, I usually get the answer: I'm a chiropractor, a doctor, a hairdresser, a tradesman, a retail store selling clothes, etc. When in fact, you are in a marketing business.

Think about it for a moment. It doesn't matter how good you are technically or how good your products and services are; if you can't get customers and sell to them, you are dead in the water. So, getting and keeping customers is critical to your business's success.

Sure, once you have a system that is getting and keeping all the customers you will ever need (more about this in Chapter 8), you can adjust your priorities accordingly.

Should you Be in Business at all?

Maybe you'll get upset with me now? But this has been my observation of business owners over many years.

I believe the main reason for this is in the book called *The E-myth Revisited* by Michael Gerber that says the would-be business owner has an "Entrepreneurial Seizure". This means that just because you are technically good at your profession, you feel you can start your own business.

The mistake is that you typically have no business owner experience, and most of your experience is just doing the technical work. Why slave away for a boss when you can have it all yourself?

SUCCESS TIP:

If you want to do the technical work, please go and work for someone else! Seriously!

You believe that by understanding how to do the business's technical work, you are entirely qualified to run a company that does that kind of work. And this is just not true.

You have had no formal training on how to be a business owner. Unbeknown to you, off you go, convinced you can do this yourself, and then you struggle for the next few years. You are trying to figure it all out.

How to carry out each role in your business. How to manage the accounting, marketing, sales, production etc.

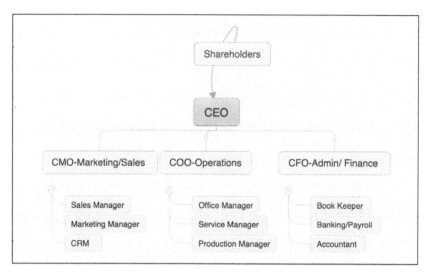

Please adjust this organisation chart to suit your business model.

So, in the scenario of a two-person business, you must decide who will be responsible for each role in the organisation chart until you get to the stage where you can hire someone else to do these roles for you. (More about how you can do this in Chapter 2.)

Of course you may not know much about using a Customer Relationship Management tool (CRM) for example…so you will have to get some help, maybe outsource parts of it.

As you can see, there is plenty to do; no wonder you're working your guts out and feeling overwhelmed just trying to make ends meet. You simply do not have all the experience required.

And frankly, it's not your fault.

You didn't know what is involved in building and running a successful and profitable business. I hope to help you with this in this book.

One of my biggest takeaways was that you must get to the stage where you "Work on your Business, not in it".

That means you work towards being the CEO of your business. Not the technician who does the work. Not the manager who manages the work being done by the technician but the CEO, working on the business, not in it.

The CEO is responsible for ensuring all the roles are completed satisfactorily. And the CEO reports to the shareholders of the business. He has to show that the company is sustainable and can offer shareholders a return on investment.

If you think of your business this way, you have every chance of success and the ability to scale your business to the point where you sell out and get the "big payday". (More about that in Chapter 9.)

Systemise Your Business

I remember way back in 2003; I was deep into systemising our trade services business. We had to document every part of the process before we could get our first sale. Two years and $100,000's later, my business partner and I were then able to start selling Trade Services Franchises.

And because everything was systemised, the franchise system worked exactly as expected. We could take a tradesperson off the street, put him into the franchise system, and in 12 months, he was doing very well. As a part of our system, we used the 3-legged stool method... Lead generation, lead conversion and client fulfilment.

As a part of the franchise system, we provided the 3-legged stool, and the tradesman did the technical work. Often just what they wanted to do.

This made so much more sense to me when I got to see Michael Gerber in person in the late 1980s. He was very forthcoming with how businesses should be operated.

I remember he told the Ray Crock MacDonalds story; from then on, my view of business changed forever.

SUCCESS TIP:

Read The Book The E-Myth Revisited by Michel Gerber. It is required reading for all my clients.

In his book *The E-myth Revisited*, Michael Gerber talks about how important it is to systemise your business BEFORE hiring someone; the role must be documented step by step. Then, you can set KPIs and deadlines for the position. That way, everything is clear.

Honestly, this was a pain in the butt, as I was already crazy busy.

But it must be done otherwise; at some point, you will just be putting "fires out" all the time.

The correct term is crisis management!

By documenting each step, you can set timeframes for each activity. Your staff will know you know how long it takes to complete all activities that make up the role.

If you don't do this, your staff will do what they know from experience. Then at some point, something goes wrong. "Why did you do it that way?" you'd say.

"Because that's the way I've always done it."

Here is a tip for you. Rather than guessing how the activities can be completed in the timeframes YOU have set, ask your staff member if they can complete them in the assigned timeframes. Yes, no, adjust to suit. Once you agree, they know what's expected, and so do you.

Also, this stops YOU from piling more work onto them. They are already busy doing what's been agreed on…nothing more.

> **SUCCESS TIP:**
>
> In my experience, it's not the person who's the problem but the system.

Power of the Mastermind

In his book *Think and Grow Rich*, Napoleon Hill described the Mastermind principle as "The coordination of knowledge and effort between two or more people who work towards a definite purpose in a spirit of harmony…no two minds ever come together without thereby creating a third, invisible, intangible force, which may be likened to a third mind", also known as the Mastermind.

What's the saying? You become like the five closest friends you hang out with? What if those friends are a part of your mastermind alliance?

Years ago, I was part of a business mastermind group in Australia, which was the best of its kind. I got so much great information and got to share what was/has worked for me. It wasn't just about taking but also freely giving information.

Communicating with people who appreciated your knowledge and would apply it was great. There is always someone with more experience in an area than you!

Please don't take this the wrong way; I mean this very sincerely. One of the hardest things I have done is finding people I like and want to hang out with.

Find a Mentor and Coach.

I cannot stress this enough. You must find a mentor you can relate to and work with. Someone who has been through what you are going through. Someone who can give you advice and guidance from their own experiences. This helps to fast-track your success.

Be open enough to ask questions and take in feedback. Then make the best decision you can and take responsibility for the decision. There is never a dumb question. A decision is better than no decision.

> **SUCCESS TIP:**
> You don't have to know what to do but know who to call.

In his book *Change your Habits, Change Your Life*, Tom Corley spent five years researching the daily habits of 233 wealthy and 128 poor individuals.

From his research, one of the rich habits of self-made millionaires was finding a mentor. Ninety-three per cent of self-made millionaires in his study who had a mentor attributed their wealth to their mentors.

Sixty-eight per cent said the mentoring they received from others was a critical factor in their success.

Where to Find Your Customers and Products to Sell?

Hopefully, you did this research before you decided to start your business. When asked this question, I usually reply, "Go where the money is in your niche."

So, look at your competitors, what they sell, and where and how they advertise online and offline. Google them, visit their website, and opt-in to any offers or promotions they have. See what emails they are sending.

One of the best things you can do at this stage is to buy one of their products. And now you are a customer. Now watch what they send you as a customer, different product offers, inserts, offers, upsells, SMS etc. This is very valuable information.

So now, during this process, you will begin to see what other products and services they offer.

One distinction to note here... the budding business owner is thinking, hey, none of my competitors is selling this product; I think it would do really well.

So, you get all excited and start looking and sourcing the product. Typically, big mistake!

There is probably a reason your competitors are not selling that product. Maybe they tried already, and it didn't work!

Don't be the Pioneer

There is a saying I learned many years ago from Dan Kennedy... "Don't be the pioneer because you'll likely be the one with the arrows in your back."

Let me explain...

If none of your competitors is selling this product, what makes you think you will successfully be able to sell this product? Chances are you will not.

It's a much better option to sell what is already selling and take some of the market that is already buying the product. And the market is already familiar with the product.

Launching a Product

In his book *Ready, Fire, Aim,* author Michael Masterson talks about the concept of velocity, going from an idea and taking action as fast as possible. But it doesn't mean taking action until you are ready.

By this, he means taking a moment and creating a short business proposal (you could use a one-page business plan here), asking questions like: Is this a good idea? Do I feel it will work? Are my revenue outcomes realistic? Do I have the money to test it? What tasks would need to be completed? Who will do those tasks? And what do I do if it doesn't work?

The way I have used this principle is to set up some marketing and do a test run first to see if YOU can sell it. And if it sells, do you make money and show a profit? If so, great. Go ahead and push the button and make/buy the product.

In my experience, though, most businesses do the opposite. First, they set everything up, buy product inventory etc. The concept of "build it and they will come" is great - if it works. But if it doesn't, you have wasted all that time, money testing and money invested in stock not selling.

They ready, aim, then fire. Much faster to fire off some tests marketing first, then take Aim if it makes sense and you make money.

Remember, it's not necessary to even have the product at this stage. Just refund the orders that come in during this test phase.

I have a good friend who is an incredible marketer. Dollar for dollar, he's the best marketer I know. When he tests ads, he places six adverts in different magazines and spends like $100K to find one or two winners. Then he makes millions…seriously!

SME Business Owner's Income Levels

According to the Australian Bureau of Statistics (ABS), the average employee income for the 2019/20 Financial Year was $52,338 per year.

According to salaryband.com, the average income of a small business owner in Australia is between $65K to $70K per year, and according to payscale.com, the average base hourly rate is $38.00.

Small business in Australia employs over 4.7 million people and 41% of the business workforce, making it Australia's biggest employer.

Typically, small business owners do not pay themselves very much or at all for the first two to three years. From an income and quality of life perspective, many would-be small business owners should consider working for someone else until their small business can afford to pay them the same employee income they would be leaving.

However, if you had the capital to invest and good cash flow well, you could take more income sooner. But most business owners tend to take what they can live on and reinvest into their business growth.

Initial and Working Capital

Your type of business determines how much capital you should have to start a business. This will make life much easier for you and reduce your chances of failure. As a rule of thumb, 80% of companies fail within the first five years. Also, being undercapitalised is a significant reason businesses run out of money and close down.

Ok, so back to the 7 Basic Business Metrics…

So let's get started. Of course, there are others, but these will do for now.

Here are seven basic key business metrics.

1. Net sales revenue
2. Gross profit and net profit
3. Sales growth rate year to date
4. Lead generation and lead conversion rate
5. Customer Lifetime Value (CLV) and Average Transaction Value (ATV)
6. Number of active customers
7. Customer and staff happiness

1. Net sales revenue

Net Sales Revenue = Gross Sales – Returns – Discounts

2. Gross profit and net profit

Gross Profit = Revenue – COGS (Cost of Goods Sold)
Net Profit = Gross profit - Expenses

3. Sales growth rate year to date

Growth Rate = Last month / Starting month x 100%

4. Lead generation and lead conversion rate

Conversion Rate = Number of sales / Number of leads

5. Customer Lifetime Value (CLV) and Average Transaction Value (ATV)

Customer Lifetime Value = Average transaction size x Average purchase frequency rate x Average customer lifetime

Average transaction value = Sales / Transactions

6. **Number of active customers**

Active customers = At Least one transaction within a specific time frame

7. **Customer and staff happiness**

Customer happiness = on a scale of 1-10, how likely are you to buy from us again?

Staff happiness – Use the staff appraisal process. Please refer to the link in the resources section of the book

The 80/20 Rule

I'm guessing you will have heard about this principle. But how many of you actively use it in your business daily?

What is the 80/20 Rule?

The 80/20 Rule, also known as the Pareto Principle, is beneficial for entrepreneurs and business owners to understand and use in their businesses. This principle states that 20% (or so) of your activities will account for 80% of your results.

How to use this Principle

Often entrepreneurs and business owners work excessive hours in their businesses to make revenue and profit. This creates a situation where your life-work balance can become unhealthy. So how can you use this principle to work to your advantage?

Find 20% of your most essential tasks that produce the highest return on investment.

So do the high-level tasks in your day first that offer the most opportunity to create the best outcome.

.

Here are some examples of the 80/20 rule in practice.

80% of your profits come from 20% of your customers
80% of problems come from 20% of customers
80% of profits come from 20% of activities
80% of your profits may come from 20% of your products
80% of your staff problems come from 20% of your staff
80% of the information you process will be mostly useless
80% of the data you get from others will not be accurate
More than 80% of the typical person's time is wasted
And we can take it a step further…

The 95/5 rule

Here are some examples of the 95/5 rule in practice.

5% of people have 95% of the money
95% of your retained wealth will come from 5% of everything you do
95% of your decisions can be wrong, and you still can get rich from completely exploiting the 5% you make right
Only 5% of things we worry about happening ever occur
Only 5% of successful people act on a solution to a problem when it presents itself
95% don't act at all

The S-Curve

One of the most important concepts I have ever seen is the S-Curve. Why? Because it will help you understand your business and product evolution on a predictable life cycle.

Understanding this concept can also help you adapt to unexpected events in your business and product lifecycle.

The 4 S-Curve Stages

Four stages have different stages of growth.

1. Initial slow growth (Early Adoption)
2. Fast growth
3. Late-stage slow growth (Maturity Point)
4. Flat or decreasing demand (Plateau and Decline)

1. Initial slow growth

In this early adoption stage, you experience slow growth as you prepare your business or product for entry into the market. If the product is a new innovative product, it will need time to be accepted by your target market. This is an excellent time to have everything in place, like having your company's logistics, operations, and enough stock to prepare for the next stage.

2. Fast growth

In this fast growth stage, your customers learn about your product via your marketing which helps you gain market share and momentum. You must scale your staffing and production accordingly to meet market expectations of speedy delivery and excellent customer service.

3. Late-stage slow growth

In this maturity stage, your product/business starts to slow. This can be due to external factors like competitors taking more market share and the product becoming a commodity based on price rather than a value proposition.

4. Flat or decreasing demand

In this final stage, your product demand and business growth are either flat or decreasing. Now, it's time to pivot and adapt by finding new and innovative products or methods.

This is called an inflection point on the S-Curve. Although an inflection point can be challenging, it's also an excellent opportunity to offer new products or a "new and improved" version of the existing winning product. Or you could try bundling the winning product with a complimentary product or selling two units as the initial sale offering a slight discount.

If this works, the business and product typically begin a new S-Curve at the initial or rapid growth stage. Happy days again.

Although the trick here is to begin the product innovation before you reach the initial product inflection point, when the initial product is selling well in the rapid growth stage, you have the following product ready to go. As one starts to drop off, the new one will take over. This will help you maintain a more constant revenue stream.

Please see the following graph.

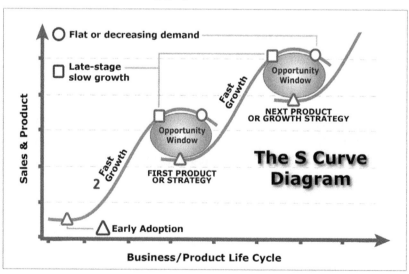

Austrade – Export Market Development Grants.

Did you know the Australian government will give you a grant to expand overseas? The amount will depend on how much your business spends on marketing etc. And yes, they will cover you for overseas flights and accommodation. Seems like a no-brainer to me.

A few hoops to jump through. But easy if you use a consultant to prepare the application and lodge it for you. There are other business grants available as well. I'll share the details in the resources section at the end of this chapter.

Action Steps:

- Apply the Key Business Metrics to your business.

- Buy, read and apply the book *The E-Myth Revisited* by Michael Gerber to your business.

- Buy and read the book *Ready, Fire, Aim* by Michael Masterson.

- Buy and read *Change your Habits, Change Your Life* by Tom Corley.

- Register for your FREE 20 min business assessment by visiting: www.TheStrategicAdvisor.com.au or email

  support@TheStrategicAdvisor.com.au

Resources:

Go to www.TheStrategicAdvisor.com.au/resources and download all the links for this chapter.

Or use your phone to scan the following QR Code:

Plus, all the links are included in the Resources Section at the end of this book.

> **"Analyse the record of any man who has accumulated a great fortune, and many of those who have accumulated modest fortunes, and you will find that they have either consciously or unconsciously employed the 'Master Mind' Principle."**
>
> **- Napoleon Hill**

CHAPTER 7

---

*Creating a Simple One-Page
Business Plan*

CHAPTER 7

Creating a Simple One-Page Business Plan

We all know how important it is to create a business plan. The problem is that we think it has to be this massive 20-page document that covers strengths, weaknesses, opportunities and threats (SWOT) etc. In my experience, this is unnecessary, especially if you are just starting your business.

Many business owners I speak to do not have a business plan. Why not, I ask? "Oh, it's just too hard, and I don't have the time". "I'm really busy, you know!"

In the early days, I was the same. I didn't want to spend time creating a plan for my business that would probably change anyway.

Then one day, I came across the concept of creating a Simple One Page Business Plan.

So, I gave it a go.

In about four hours, you can knock out a good business plan using a basic template. Don't dwell too much on the details; include the basics and adjust later.

This business plan is a concise and straightforward summary of your goals.

It typically includes key elements such as a mission statement, your target market, unique value proposition, marketing and sales plans, and financial projections; all consolidated into a single page.

A business plan provides a quick overview of where you want your business to grow, making it easy to communicate this to all stakeholders in your company, including staff.

Your business will become your roadmap to follow and build on as it grows. And as your business grows, you'll get accurate information like sales revenue, profits, selling channels, etc., that you use to update your business plan accordingly.

Don't be surprised if something you thought would do well bombs out. And other things are a winner. It is simply the 80/20 rule at work.

For me, there is a more significant reason why I like using a business plan. It's called setting your intentions. By putting this information down on paper, I believe you are putting it out there for the universe to send back to you.

The benefits of using a simple one-page business plan.

Using a one-page business plan has many benefits for you and your business.

#1 Simplicity: A one-page business plan is easy to use and understand.

#2 Focus: Only one page forces you to clarify and simplify your ideas. This helps you stay focused on what's important.

#3 Quick Reference: You can refer to it quickly and make changes easily.

#4 Flexibility: It can be adapted and updated as needed.

#5 Clarity: A one-page business plan is concise and transparent, making it easier to communicate your vision to all stakeholders.

#6 Time Saving: Creating and reviewing a one-page business plan takes less time than a more detailed multi-page one.

How to create a simple one-page business plan

Here are the steps in creating a one-page business plan using a vision, a mission, setting objectives, the strategy, and key objectives.

Step #1: Create your Vision Statement

The first step in creating a one-page business plan is articulating your vision. The vision statement is a brief and inspiring statement that defines what you hope to achieve with your business in the next 12-24 months.

It sets the tone for the entire plan and provides a clear direction for your business. When creating a vision statement, it's crucial to consider your company's values, aspirations, and purpose. Your vision should be concise, memorable, and easy to understand.

Step #2: Create your Mission Statement

The next step is to create a mission statement. The mission statement defines the purpose of your business and explains what it does, whom it serves, and what problem it solves. It guides a clear understanding of your company's offerings and the value it brings to your customers. And statement should be simple, concise, and aligned with your vision.

Step #3: Set your Objectives

Once you have defined your vision and mission, it's time to set your objectives. Objectives should be specific, measurable, achievable, relevant, and time-bound (SMART).

This should align with your vision and mission and provide a clear understanding of what you want to achieve. Objectives should cover various areas, such as growth, profitability, customer satisfaction and more.

Step #4: Develop your Strategy

The next step is to develop a strategy for achieving your objectives. The plan should outline the tactics, activities, and initiatives you will use to reach your goals. It should align with your vision and mission and clearly show how you plan to achieve your desired outcome. When creating a strategy, it's essential to think about your strengths, weaknesses, opportunities and threats (SWOT analysis).

Step #5: Identify your Key Metrics

Identifying key metrics or KPIs is essential in creating a one-page business plan. Key metrics are quantitative measures that you use to track the progress of your business. They provide a clear understanding of what success looks like and allow you to measure your strategy's impact.

Key metrics should be relevant, measurable, and actionable. They should be aligned with your objectives and provide a clear understanding of what you hope to achieve.

Step #6: Organise and Present.

The final step is to organise and present your one-page business plan clearly and concisely. The layout should be simple, clean, and visually appealing font should be easy to read, and the language should be simple and concise. I like to use bullet points to make the plan easy to read, understand, and act on.

Check out the following simple one-page example, and there will be a template you can download from the website.

The Simple Business Plan for:
Company Name Jan - Dec 2023.

VISION

What are you building? (2-5 yrs.)

Mission

Why does your business exist?

OBJECTIVES

What are your specific measures?

STRATEGY

How are you going to build your company?

BUSINESS PLAN

What is the work to be done?

Action Steps:

- Download and complete the Simple One Page Business Plan by visiting the resources section on the website.

- Set aside some time and complete your one-page business plan.

- Register for your FREE 20min assessment by visiting:

  www.TheStrategicAdvisor.com.au or email support@ TheStrategicAdvisor.com.au

Resources:
Go to www.TheStrategicAdvisor.com.au/resources and download all the links for this chapter.

Or use your phone to scan the following QR Code:

Plus, all the links are included in the Resources Section at the end of this book.

> **❝**
> *"Focus on doing what's important first, not what's urgent, to achieve your goals faster."*
>
> *- Stephen Covey*

CHAPTER 8

Speed2Profits™ Business Building Program

CHAPTER 8

Speed2Profits™ Business Building Program

In 2008, a good friend, Alexi Neocleous, owner of Fubbi.co, asked me to listen to this business program. I thought oh no, not another business program. Anyway, lucky for me, I followed his advice. I'm glad I did. The program was excellent.

Simple and easy to understand. Great methods to build and scale your business. That is just what I was looking for. I knew about some of the content already. But the way the information was broken down and taught made this program stand out. I can tell you I have bought many programs in the past that I didn't finish. But this one I did finish.

I was so impressed that I contacted the owner of the program. I filled out his pre-call questionnaire. Then we scheduled a Profit Optimization session.

Ten minutes into the session, he nailed my business. It was like he'd been working with me for ages. So, we identified the most significant opportunities in the business and set some action steps to take - a very valuable session.

Scott Hallman, the creator of *Speed2Profits™*, is super street-smart and a really nice guy. I thought I had to get this guy to coach me. He agreed, and so our friendship began.

Seeing how Scott and I have been friends for so long, he's agreed to give you a sneak peek into the full-blown *Speed2Profits™ Program*. It is called *"The 5-Day Profit Acceleration Blueprint Program"*. It has frequently been a core training at $10,000 per person business events.

I hope this valuable gem will help transform your business with a skill you will carry forward in your business life.

The *5-day Profit Acceleration Blueprint Program*

In a few minutes a day, over 5 days, you will create your customised revenue profit and business wealth acceleration model. By completing this short program, you will learn how to increase your profitability PREDICTABLY by 10 to 50% or more. This can be accomplished without spending extra money on marketing sales or different technology.

You will also get access to the program's proprietary *ProfitCalculator™*, which will help track your results and Return on Investment. Usually, this is only available in the full version of the program.

At a very high level, the 5-day program focuses on maximising your lead to clients, customers, or patients. Then your customers' lifetime value. This is where you will likely generate most of your revenue and profits from your repeat customers. This is an essential component of this program.

What's included in the *5-day Profit Acceleration Blueprint Program?*

The training includes the first of eight modules of the full-blown *Speed2Profits™ Program.*

The 5-day program includes eight videos to guide you step by step to completing your powerful *Profit Acceleration Blueprint.*

Each video is designed to be about 7 to 15 minutes long and delivered in bite-sized chunks so you can assimilate it and take action. This is really important!

Imagine knowing how you can add 10-50%+ in profits to your business by spending just a few minutes a day for one week. Then imagine taking the precise actions to make this a reality!

This program is easily worth $1,000. I have arranged to get it to you for free. With that said, please do not discount the value of this content or fail to complete the program.

The link to access this program will be in the Action Steps at the end of this chapter.

But before we continue, who is Scott Hallman?

Scott Hallman's companies have twice been named to the *Prestigious Inc. Magazine's* "Inc. 500" list of the fastest-growing privately held companies in America (#59 and #106), starting from the ground up.

He also co-founded an IT Consulting company that grew from $0 to $85M in just 21 months and a year later reached a market value of $1 Billion.

Scott is a world-leading business growth trainer focusing on Business Growth Optimization. He has consulted with Tony Robbins, Chet Holmes, leading Internet marketers, Spartan Race's CEO, Joe DeSena, Sandler Training CEO, David Mattson, Yanik Silver, multiple Inc. 500 ranking companies, and businesses in over 250 industries around the world.

Scott's book, *The 7 Success Drivers To HYPERGROWTH*, was a #1 Amazon / Kindle bestseller.

Scott has been a frequent speaker at leading business events, including Tony Robbins' Business Mastery, GKIC's SuperSummit, and several Jay Abraham events, for audiences of up to 7,000 business owners.

Scott realised not everyone could pay him thousands of dollars a month, plus share in the upside, for private coaching, so he did the next best thing and created the *Speed2Profits™ Program* so any business could benefit from his success strategies.

Once you complete the *5-Day Profit Acceleration Blueprint Program,* I am convinced you will race to get the full-blown *Speed2Profits™ Program.*

The Full Program Overview

You will take the *10 ProfitDrivers™* you created in your *Profit Blueprint* and dive into 257 specific strategies and tactics in *Speed2Profits™ Program* to help you create the results from your Blueprint.

Scott shows you the true Power of OPTIMIZATION… and how to apply it to your marketing, sales, and client value processes (everything involved in getting more clients and maximising their transactional value for life). And, if you are in the early stages of your business, you will learn to maximise your cash flow profits from day one to optimise your growth.

Don't Make This Common Mistake…"Teach Me Something New"

Beware of the "Teach Me Something New Syndrome" as you go through this program. That is the continual search for some Magic Pill that will cure your problems and skyrocket your growth overnight. It is a dangerous pill that keeps the vast majority of businesses from achieving the level of success they deserve.

If you have found yourself chasing this Magic Pill, you likely have experienced continual frustration, disappointment, and wasted money chasing this quick fix.

Back to The Program

With that said, I want to assure you that in addition to learning how to OPTIMIZE what you already are doing, you will also discover dozens of "new" strategies and tactics for improving and building your business in the *Speed2Profits™ Program*. The key distinction is that these "new" ideas will be proven, tested success strategies that are simple to execute, and require little time, money or effort.

Over the course of the full-blown program, you will learn how to predictably and systematically increase your business profits 25-

100%+, faster and easier than you ever thought possible. All without any specialised skills, added resources, fancy technology or investment. You will learn how to create a simple yet powerful Model that will enable you to implement and execute even more effectively than you do today. A model is built using your business's actual financial and conversion figures.

This will determine the predictable revenue and profit you generate from the *Speed2Profits™ Program.*

This Profit Model will also contain the precise strategies and tactics you will utilise to generate these added profits for your business. By the time the program is done...

- You will have a clear strategy and execution plan for methodically implementing each success strategy and tactic within your unique business.

- You will learn to identify your business' Profit Drivers or measurable steps in your marketing, sales, and customer value processes. The *Speed2Profits™ Program* covers *10 ProfitDrivers™* we'll go over in detail.

- You will also learn HOW to predictably increase your revenue and profit by "one-upping" the current performance of these *ProfitDrivers™* by just 3-5% each.

- You will learn to make these small performance-boosting improvements with precision, collectively creating geometric growth resulting from the Law of Compounding.

SUCCESS TIP:

A Profit Driver is any step in your marketing, sales, or ongoing client conversion processes that can be measured and improved to increase performance.

Each week you will produce measurable and ever-increasing revenue and profit increases as you progress.

And it doesn't stop there.

Business Wealth and Your Retirement Fund

Making significant profits year in and year out is fantastic. Building wealth is even better.

Our business represents the key to building wealth and funding our retirement for many of us. When we're ready to enter that chapter of our lives, there may be no Social Security retirement fund. I'm not saying it won't, but I'd rather bet on something I can control than something I can't.

Therefore, in the *Speed2Profits™ Program*, you will also learn how to turn these newfound profit streams into BUSINESS WEALTH, adding hundreds of thousands and even millions of dollars to your company's value.

It's ALL About IMPLEMENTATION

It is critically important for you to understand that the intense focus on IMPLEMENTATION makes the *Speed2Profits™ Program* so different. I have no interest in teaching you a bunch of "new" strategies and tactics that get added to the stack of ideas that someday will hopefully get implemented.

In contrast, the *Speed2Profits™ Program* provides you with strategies and tactics you can quickly implement, complete with the detailed step-by-step implementation and execution system proven to produce measurable results and lock these in place over the customer's life.

You will end the Intensive Core Training period with a completely different view of what it takes to succeed in the short and long-term. Plus, have a detailed action plan for the balance of the year.

The *Speed2Profits™ Program* includes an intensive online members-only Learning Centre, nearly a year in the making. It has all the training modules, transcripts, action guides, and success templates for every module. Business case studies include the breakthroughs these businesses have experienced and the precise strategies and tactics they utilised.

The program was designed so that ANY business, regardless of industry, size, geography, or level of expertise, can effectively implement what they learn with little time, money or effort.

I am confident that once you see how simple it is to achieve these performance improvements for each of the *ProfitDrivers™*, utilising the Right Strategies and the Right Execution process, you will find yourself, for perhaps the first time, implementing at the Speed of Sound and instantly producing measurable revenue and profit increases as you may never have thought possible.

The *Speed2Profits™ Program* also makes implementation and execution within your company something your team looks forward to, providing them with a sense of certainty and rewarding accomplishment. That is because it is so EASY to do with the proprietary system.

The Ultimate Competitive Advantage

We, business owners, are in an unprecedented competitive environment, with more sophisticated, broader reaching, hungry, and at times desperate competitors.

The pace of change is accelerating at ever-increasing speeds, and therefore we must be able to adapt to these changes and become and remain the leader in our space. Learning HOW to effectively OPTIMIZE your new client generation and customer transactional value and manage your business SYSTEMATICALLY will provide you with the ultimate competitive advantage.

The *Speed2Profits™ Program* takes implementation to a new level by integrating the *Dynamic Learning System*. Dynamic Learning involves continually modifying your Success Formulas and procedures to adapt to changing customer needs, the competitive environment, and the economy to ensure you stay ahead of the pack and dominate your market for years to come.

Your competitors will scramble to keep up with you as you "dynamically" modify your Success Formulas, constantly improving everything you do, and stay in front of them long-term.

Fastest Way to Build a Great Company

Optimisation of your marketing, sales, and client value processes is only one component of building a great business. In addition, you must continually innovate, adapt and find new ways of attracting leads; have solid financial and management systems; provide quality products and services that businesses and consumers need; build strong teams; utilise state-of-the-art technology and a host of other fundamentals.

There is no faster, more predictable, or easier way to increase your cash profits than deploying The Power of OPTIMIZATION. It generates the needed money to hire the best talent…deploy the best technology…hire the best marketers, and more.

Here's some bonus Content from the full-blown *Speed2Profits™ Program.*

The 4 sure fire ways to get all the customers you will ever need.

#1 - Speed of Response. (Video 2-3)

This can be a critical strategy for many businesses because these prospects often will have contacted your competitors as well, and often the first to respond will win.

When an interested prospect responds to your marketing efforts, it is critical that you're able to REACH/CONNECT with them as quickly as possible.

Even a 30-minute delay can cause them to seek an alternative company to purchase their desired product or service.

#2 - Increase the Number of Follow-up Attempts (Video 2-4)

As I said earlier, when you could not answer the phone live, interact via chat or email, or in person, or get the person to engage in watching your video, listening to your audio, or reading your sales letter, literature, or detailed specifications.

Therefore, this requires repeated attempts before you can connect with most of the leads you could not handle live.

The first few days, weeks, or months for some products or services are likely when the prospect is in what's called a Purchase State. They are focused on purchasing or learning about a particular product or service. At the very minimum, you should contact a lead at least seven times. After all, they may not respond immediately because their need is not that urgent, or they may already be speaking with your competitors, or decided to hold off, or got distracted.

Studies show that 81% of sales happen after the 5th contact, some say after the 7th contact, and yet 85% of businesses stop after 1-2 attempts/ contacts.

#3 - Increase the Number of Mediums or Communication Methods (Video 2-5)

You should follow up with more than one medium or method of contact. So if someone gives you a phone number and an email address, you should contact the prospect in both those mediums. Make sense?

I know it sounds logical, but many businesses do not follow this simple tactic, so I want to ensure you're not one of them.

Using more than one medium or communication method can significantly increase the number of prospects you get to engage with.

Even if you only have their email, you can still communicate in multiple methods using additional touch types. What do I mean by that? You can use text, pictures, audio, and video to maximise the number of leads that ultimately engage in Meaningful Communication with you.

#4 – Utilize Compelling Incentives to Motivate Prospects to Communicate With You (Video 2-6)

Ok, you have followed up rapidly and diligently, utilising multiple mediums. So how else can you increase Meaningful Communication performance even further?

The answer is… Offer Compelling Incentives.

Compelling Incentives can produce profound results in any business. A Compelling Incentive is any value-added offer that motivates a prospect to take some action. It distinguishes you from your competitors and makes it easy for them to respond to your marketing.

These include various forms of free offers, bonuses, and price incentives used to:

- Increase leads
- Increase meaningful communications
- Increase sales engagements
- Increase sales conversion
- Increase the frequency of repurchases
- Increase the number of products or services sold
- Increase pricing

- Increase upsells and cross-sells
- Increase referrals
- Increase customer loyalty and
- Increase the reactivation of past customers as well

Deploying the Power of Scarcity is one key to making Compelling Incentives even more effective. This can include bonuses, special terms, or pricing available only if they take action now!

Business Growth Success Vault

To further ensure your success, Scott has emptied his Business Growth Success Vault, filled with in-the-trenches, proven success strategies and tactics for over 30 years of business experience. It also includes some painful yet invaluable learning lessons that will help you avoid many costly mistakes he made over the years.

This Success Vault contains the secrets that have helped his companies get ranked on the Inc. 500 list of the fastest growing privately held companies in America, not once but twice, and helped him build another business, with his co-founder, from the ground up into a billion-dollar valued company within just 21 months.

The Opportunity of a Lifetime

His private clients pay him $40,000-$120,000 retainers per year to access this Success Vault and get his coaching on which ones to deploy, when to deploy them, and how to implement them within their unique business and environment most effectively.

And now, for the first time, Scott is including the Business Growth Success Vault in the *Speed2Profits™ Program* with those of you who invest in the full program.

Access to the full blown *Speed2Profits™ Program* is available by application only.

For more information, please send an email to: support@TheStategicAdvisor.com.au

Action Steps:

- Register for the *5-Day Profit Acceleration Blueprint Program:* **5DayProfitBlueprintNow.com**

Or use your phone to scan the following QR Code:

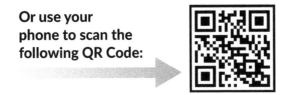

- Register for your FREE 20min business assessment by visiting: www.TheStrategicAdvisor.com.au or email support@TheStrategicAdvisor.com.au

Resources:

Go to www.TheStrategicAdvisor.com.au/resources and download all the links for this chapter.

Or use your phone to scan the following QR Code:

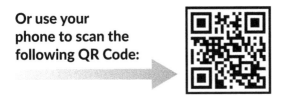

Plus, all the links are included in the Resources Section at the end of this book.

"There is no faster, more predictable, or easier way to increase your cash profits than deploying The Power of OPTIMIZATION."

- Scott Hallman.

CHAPTER 9

Build Your Business to Sell

CHAPTER 9

Build Your Business to Sell

In 2006 my business partner and I owned a business called Aircon Direct. This business sold air conditioning split systems online and offline all-around Australia. It was a unique model at the time. Many thought it couldn't be done. But you know what? It worked—selling big clunky air conditioning units from our base in Sydney.

We were getting up to 50 leads a day. So many, that we had to outsource the calls to a call centre. And call them back as soon as we could. Some days we were selling up to $20,000 per day. Customers would get their order in a few days and save up to $600 by buying from Aircon Direct instead of buying locally.

Initially, we built the business to help improve the buying power of another division in our group of companies. But very quickly, it became a stand-alone business. And I got really busy really fast. In fact, I couldn't handle it, so we decided to sell it.

This business was built and sold in 9 months for a 6-figure sum.

How did this happen?

Looking back, because we had spent so much time systemising our trade services business and converting it into a franchise, we subconsciously built up the company using the 3-legged stool method I discussed in Chapter 6.

If you remember, the 3-legged stool method consists of lead generation, lead conversion and client fulfilment.

Therefore, all the other pieces fell into place because the 3-legged stool method was set up and working.

Why am I telling you this?

If you have all the correct elements up and running in your business, it's straightforward to exit your business and get the maximum amount possible.

In the case of Aircon Direct, the 50 leads a day was what the buyer mostly wanted. Of course, the revenue and the website were significant as well.

To this day, the buyer and I are very good friends.

SUCCESS TIP:

I have this saying... When's the best time to Sell Something? Usually, when you don't want to. For example the business making good money or the car that still looks nice and shiny.

Beginning with the End in Mind in your Business.

You should envision the end goal for YOU and your business from the beginning.

Because my preferred business exit strategy is to "build to sell", that is what I am going to focus on here.

So you wish to sell your business in the future. Therefore, you build the company so it will be attractive to the future buyer, and you continually work towards achieving this outcome throughout the life of your business.

This means you have a good business model, unique products, a loyal customer base and a competitive edge.

This includes documenting and systemising every part of your business.

Also, what a future buyer will be looking for is that YOU are not in the day-to-day operations of your business. This means you have built a team and that "one significant other" is running your business for you. Your 2IC. Your General Manager.

Plus, the benefit of having that "one significant other" person is that you get to take a holiday and be confident that the business is still running as if you were there. You can switch off and enjoy yourself.

What I used to do when my business partner wanted some time off I would keep a journal of what happened day to day. So, when he returned, we would sit down and go through what happened. He'd get up to speed. Then I would take some time off, and he would do the same. It worked very well. This way, we didn't have to talk to each other while on leave unless it was an emergency.

What's Your Number?

Selling your business is a massive payday for you. One of the biggest in your life. So what's your number? How much do you want? Do you want enough to retire or take a break for a couple of years and then go again? All very important questions.

If you want a $1,000,000 payout, your business will have to show a profit of about $300 to $350K of Seller Discretionary Earnings (SDE). Roughly a 3X Earning Multiple.

This multiple can go up or down depending on your business model, recurring ongoing income, and other factors like how extensive and active your database is, plus things like average transaction size and your customer's lifetime value. (More on this in Chapter 6.)

Seller Discretionary Earnings (SDE) is the term both buyer and seller use to agree on calculating the profit figure. Therefore, SDE is the profit of what your buyer can expect after the sale is completed. Working out the SDE figure will result in several "add-backs" that will improve your profit figure from what your financials look like monthly.

An example is any owner-related expenses that the business pays, like travel, car leases, and owner salaries (in some cases), which are classed as add-backs. Any costs the new owner will not incur after selling the business are classed as an add-back.

Another form of add-backs is significant one-time expenses like building a website for $15,000. From my personal experience, this figure can add up and surprise you.

Be Conscious of What You Are Spending On in Your Business.

Something to think about at this point if you are building your business to sell, watch what you spend on your business that does not drop to the bottom line as profit or could be agreed as an SDE.

For example, testing multiple products and new marketing for those products will be considered a business expense, not an add-back. Remember the 80/20 rule. Find your winners and maximise profits rather than extensive testing. Another example can be spending money on unnecessary business branding that is hard to measure and often shows little to no return on investment.

This is where the *Speed2Profits*™ is beneficial, as it shows you how to improve on what is already working rather than trying new forms of marketing.

SUCCESS TIP:

Regularly Ask your Accountant to work out what your business is worth by adding back the add-backs.

How Do You Build Your Business to Sell?

Building your business to sell requires a combination of strategic planning and taking action.

Here are some critical steps to consider:

- Ensure you develop a range of products (or services) your market wants / needs. You should also have a strong value proposition and brand that sets you apart from your competition. And you can show ongoing revenues and profits.

- Create a business that is scalable. This allows for expansion and growth that can increase the value of your business.

- Build a good team behind you. As I said earlier, finding that "one significant other" can be a major factor in getting the most for your business because you will attract potential buyers who want to be investors. Not work in the company.

- Having documented systems and processes shows that your business is scalable, just like a franchise model.

- Have a diversified revenue stream. This can help buffer against different market fluctuations, such as a new aggressive competitor entering your market.

- Focus on creating raving fans in your business. This demonstrates that your company has a proven track record of outstanding customer satisfaction.

- Constantly monitor your niche. Look for new market trends and what your competitors are doing. This will help you to spot new opportunities and stay ahead of the S-Curve (More on the S-Curve in Chapter 6.)

- Be prepared to sell. Having excellent and up-to-date financial records will show your business's current value. Remember to keep in mind that you want to sell your business.

- Leave some money on the table for the new owner. This means you have a list of products, markets, and methods you have identified and documented as part of your business plan that you haven't got to yet. And a value of what this would be worth to the business if implemented—untapped potential.

SUCCESS TIP:

Leave Some Money On the Table for the New Owner

The Founder Factor.

From my personal "in the trenches" experience, this is my take on the term "Founder Factor".

The founder of the business can have a significant impact on the success and growth of the company. This include factors such as the founder's vision, passion, leadership, and ability to take action on their ideas. And their role in shaping the company's strategy and overall direction is so important, especially during the early stages of the growth of the business.

The founder is often willing to take on more risks and try new things. This can be great for a new business in the early stages and help find new growth opportunities.

The founder has a strong sense of ownership and can be very committed to the business's success. Which means they will spend much of their time, day and night, doing what is required to make the business successful. This can also be the start of founder burnout.

But the founder can become a liability when the business gets to a certain size. What I mean here is that the founder or founders need to gain the skill set, expertise or experience to take the business to the next level.

The founder can resist change, especially if they have a strong emotional attachment to their business. This is their baby.

At this stage, the business typically requires capital injection and a good team with the knowledge and experience to take the company to the next level.

SUCCESS TIP:

Sell some of your business and take on someone who has the required abilities to grow the company to the next level.

So, what happens? If the Founders can realise their limitations and step aside and allow more strategic decisions to be made by their team. Great.

If not, the business will eventually implode. The culture of the business will start to suffer, staff will begin to leave, sales will begin to fall, and the company will spiral downwards. You will eventually trash the business.

Please do not let this happen to you!

How? By having a clear exit strategy. This will help you to determine what you will and won't do for money, how many staff you want and how big you want your business to be.

Action Steps:

- Register for your FREE 20min business assessment by visiting:

    www.TheStrategicAdvisor.com.au or email

    support@TheStrategicAdvisor.com.au

Resources:

Go to www.TheStrategicAdvisor.com.au/resources and download all the links for this chapter.

Or use your phone to scan the following QR Code:

Plus, all the links are included in the Resources Section at the end of this book.

> ❝
> ## *"Begin by Always Expecting Good Things To Happen. "*
>
> ## *- Tom Hopkins*

CHAPTER 10

Bringing it All Together

CHAPTER 10

Bringing it All Together

Ok, so where to from here?

We have covered a lot in this book. It's different from your usual business book. This book is a holistic guide for business owners looking to fast-track their success and create lasting change in their personal and business lives.

As I said in the introduction, I wish I had had a book like this when I started my first business over 30 years ago.

I'm sure you now realise how important it is to change your inner world as fast as possible so you will begin seeing more significant and better changes in your outer world.

So now you have a head start. Learn from my mistakes years ahead of time.

As I have said throughout the book, you must take action. You must do more than just read the book to help you.

Taking action means doing something different and outside of your comfort zone.

Taking action means looking at where you are now and where you'd like to be personally and in your business within the next 12 months.

Taking action means investing time and money into yourself to grow.

Remember the definition of insanity? Doing the same thing over and over again and expecting a different result. I'm saying this for my benefit as well as yours.

Here are five things you can do to get off to a Fast Start right now.

1. Register for your FREE 20 min personal call
2. Find out your numerology Life Path number and where you are in your 9-year numerology cycle of life. Begin to go with the "flow of life"
3. Register for Free 5-day access to the Speed2Profits business-building program
4. Download your free Heath Report by Dr Wayne Pickstone
5. Go to Kolbe.com, complete and download your personal Kolbe A™ Index assessment

Please remember it doesn't have to end here with this book. We are here for you. If you get stuck or have questions, you can contact my team and me directly by emailing:

support@TheStrategicAdvisor.com.au

I've had a wonderful time sharing my experiences with you. I would love to hear your thoughts on the book and how you applied this information to your business. Feel free to share by sending me an email.

Here's to Creating a Better you,

Michael Fullick

Some of the key takeaways from the book

- How beliefs acquired during your childhood can shape your reality as an adult.

- How the *Wealth Conditioning Program for Business Owners* can be used to clarify your current beliefs and attitudes and then upgrade your belief system for maximum success.

- Use the *Kolbe A™* Index assessment tool to find out what you are naturally good at when you take action.

- Why it's essential to focus on your natural strengths and abilities when you take action and delegate everything else to increase productivity and avoid burnout.

- Knowing your numerology numbers allows you to make better personal and business decisions and "go with the flow" of life.

- Money and happiness are not always correlated, and it's important to find a balance between work, money and life and nurturing relationships for overall well-being.

- What you will and won't do for money and happiness in your life.

- Practicing gratitude is also vital in finding happiness, as it helps you focus on what you already have instead of what you lack.

- Taking time out of your day to sit quietly and meditate can dramatically improve your well-being.

- Prioritising your health and well-being has a vital role to play in your life and business.

- Using the "One Weird Technique" is key to excellent health and long-term success.

- Testing out a product first before launching the product using the Ready Fire Aim concept.

- By NOT experiencing an "Entrepreneurial Seizure", you give yourself the best opportunity for success.

- Using the 80/20 principle, find 20% of your most important tasks that produce the highest return on investment.

- How a Simple One Page Business plan is helpful for quickly summarising your business ideas and strategy clearly and concisely.

- The Speed2Profits Business Building Program is a comprehensive business growth training program designed to help you optimise your marketing and sales without spending any extra money on marketing.

- Building your business to sell is a very profitable way to make a lot of money.

- Remember to download all your FREE resources by visiting: **www.TheStrategicAdvisor.com.au/resources**

Or use your phone to scan the following QR Code:

"Create the better you, each day anew,
Grow beyond what you already knew,
Believe in yourself and all you can do,
And watch your dreams and goals come
true."

- Michael Fullick

RESOURCES

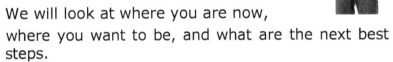
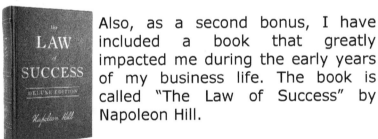

HIRE RIGHTFIT™ TALENT

Expand by identifying the right person for the role.
Reduce costly turnover and build productive teams
with RightFit.

Identify whether the candidate is a good fit for the job and the supervisor, with our EEOC compliant process.

1 Define Role Requirements & Supervisor Compatibility

The supervisor of the role takes the Kolbe A™
Index to identify their natural strengths,
and the Kolbe C™ Index to identify the
strengths required in the role.

2 Build a Job Profile

The supervisor's Kolbe A, and the C Index
results are combined to create a Kolbe Range
of Success™ Report. This report identifies the
ideal range for candidate's Kolbe A result for
the role.

3 Screen Candidates

The Kolbe RightFit software compares the
candidate's Kolbe A result against the Range of
Success Report created for the role to generate
a Candidate Report with an A to F grade.

ADDITIONAL RESOURCES

Go to www.TheStrategicAdvisor.com.au/resources and download all the links for each chapter.

Or use your phone to scan the following QR Code:

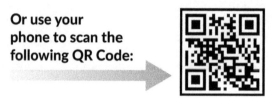

Plus, all the links are added here for each chapter.

It may be hard to access the links from the book as some are long.

But I have included them here so you can use this section as a checklist when you download them from the resources link on the website.

Chapter 1 – Wealth Conditioning Program for Business Owners.

1. Complete *The Wealth Conditioning Questionnaire for Business Owners.*

2. Register for your FREE 20 min assessment to see how you can register for the Wealth Conditioning Program for Business Owners by visiting:

   www.TheStrategicAdvisor.com.au or email

   support@TheStrategicAdvisor.com

   • Books: *Conversations with God* by Neale Donald Walsch Books.

   AU
   https://www.booktopia.com.au/conversations-with-god-neale-donald-walsch/book/9780733611957.html

USA
https://www.amazon.com/Conversations-Neale-Donald-Walsch-Collection/dp/9123797223

- Watch the demo Video. *How does muscle testing work?* Please visit the resources section of the website.

- Watch *Rewrite Your MIND* (40 Million Bits/Second) | Dr Bruce Lipton's *It Takes 15 Minutes.* https://www.youtube.com/watch?v=eB-vh6VWdcM&t=70s

- Watch Dr Bruce Lipton Explains *How To Reprogram Your Subconscious Mind.* https://www.youtube.com/watch?v=OqLT_CNTNYA&t=17s

Chapter 2 – What You are Naturally Good At When you Take Action?

- Complete your Kolbe A™ Index and download the report. **https://shop.kolbe.com/product/kolbe-a-index**

  https://www.kolbe.com/the-kolbe-system/

Or use your phone to scan the following QR Code:

- Watch: https://poweredbyinstinct.com/episode/stop-hiring-smart-likable-people-finding-the-rightfit-for-the-roles-in-your-company

- Once you have your Kolbe A score, see how to activate it: https://www.youtube.com/watch?v=jBvKkcmlRFI&t=1s

- Remote Staff Seat Lease Enquiry, please email: support@TheStrategicAdvisor.com.au

Chapter 3 – The Power of Knowing Your Numbers.

- Work out your Life Path number and Personal Year number by visiting:

https://www.peacefulwarrior.com/life-purpose-calculator/

**Or use your
phone to scan the
following QR Code:**

- Book: *The Complete Book of Numerology* by David Phillips.

AU
https://www.booktopia.com.au/the-complete-book-of-numerology-david-a-phillips/book/9781401907273.html

USA
https://www.amazon.com/Complete-Book-Numerology-David-Phillips/dp/140190727X

- Book: *The Life you were born to Live* by Dan Millman

AU
https://www.booktopia.com.au/the-life-you-were-born-to-live-dan-millman/book/9781932073751.html

USA
https://www.amazon.com/Life-Were-Born-Revised-Anniversary/dp/1932073752

Chapter 4 – Money and Happiness.

- Download and listen to *Abraham Hick's Meditations* every day.

  AU
  https://www.booktopia.com.au/getting-into-the-vortex-esther-and-jerry-hicks/book/9781401962111.html

  USA
  https://www.amazon.com/Getting-into-Vortex-Meditations-Attraction/dp/1401961827

- Book: *The Silva Method* by Jose Silva and Philip Miele

  AU
  https://www.booktopia.com.au/the-silva-mind-control-method-jose-silva/book/9781982185602.html

  USA
  https://www.amazon.com/Silva-Mind-Control-Method-Revolutionary/dp/1982185600

- Access the free Happiness Online Course by visiting:
  https://www.coursera.org/learn/the-science-of-well-being

Chapter 5 – Some Straight Talk about Your Health and Well-Being as a Business Owner.

- To get your free digital downloads and webinar, please go to:
  https://onpurposeentrepreneur.com

  Or use your phone to scan the following QR Code:

- If you wish to contact Dr Wayne Pickstone directly, please send an email to: support@onpurposeentrepreneur.com

  To learn more about foods that may cause and prevent chronic inflammation and oxidative stress, please visit:

  https://onpurposeentrepreneur.com.

- Download the example meal plan and list of foods PDF by visiting:

  www.TheStrategicAdvisor.com.au/resources

- Watch the *4-minute workout* video by Dr Zach Bush MD
  https://www.youtube.com/watch?v=PwJCJToQmps

- Watch the video by Dr Mercola, *Nitric Oxide Release Workout*
  https://www.youtube.com/watch?v=qEui9ImJaiI

References
- https://starmicronics.com/blog/top-5-reasons-why-small-businesses-fail/

  https://www.cnbc.com/2017/11/14/richest-1-percent-now-own-half-the-worlds-wealth.html

Chapter 6 – Let's Talk About Your Business

- Register for your FREE 20min business assessment by visiting: www.TheStrategicAdvisor.com.au or email support@TheStrategicAdvisor.com.au

- Book: *Ready, Fire, Aim* by Michael Masterson

  AU
  https://www.booktopia.com.au/ready-fire-aim-michael-masterson/book/9781119086857.html

  USA
  https://www.amazon.com/Ready-Fire-Aim-Million-Agora/dp/111908685X

- Book: *The E-Myth Revisited* by Michael Gerber

  AU
  https://www.booktopia.com.au/the-e-myth-revisited-michael-e-gerber/book/9780887307287.html

  USA
  https://www.amazon.com/Myth-Revisited-Small-Businesses-About/dp/0887307280

- Watch *The E-Myth* - Key-note lecture by Michael E. Gerber
  https://www.youtube.com/watch?v=XP3wm63KS8E

- Watch Napoleon Hill – *Mastermind Principle*
  https://www.youtube.com/watch?v=XMzu0ZzyIFo

- **Austrade Consultant:** Rod Campbell & Associates Pty Ltd
  rod@busgrant.com.au +61 2 92415900 or +61419405091

- Austrade – Export Market Development Grants.
  https://www.austrade.gov.au/australian/export/export-grants

- **Business Grants:**
  https://www.thegrantshub.com.au/
  https://help.grants.gov.au/

- **Customer happiness app:**
  https://www.hubspot.com/customer-satisfaction

- Download the Staff Appraisal PDFs by visiting:
  www.TheStrategicAdvisor.com.au/resources

Chapter 7 - Creating a Simple One-Page Business Plan.

- Download your Simple One Page Business Plan by visiting:
  www.TheStrategicAdvisor.com.au/resources

- Free One page Business Plan Templates

  https://www.smartsheet.com/content/one-page-business-plan-templates

- Book: *The One Page Business Plan* by Jim Horan

  AU

  https://www.booktopia.com.au/the-one-page-business-plan-jane-horan/book/9781906465315.html

  USA
  https://www.amazon.com/Page-Business-Plan-Creative-Entrepreneur/dp/1658185374

Chapter #8 - *Speed2Profits*™ Business Building Program

- Register for the *5-Day Profit Acceleration Blueprint Program*:

5DayProfitBlueprintNow.com

**Or use your
phone to scan the
following QR Code:**

- Register for your FREE 20 min business assessment by visiting:

  www.TheStrategicAdvisor.com.au or email

  support@TheStrategicAdvisor.com.au

Chapter 9 – Build your Business to Sell

- Register for your FREE 20min business assessment by visiting:

  www.TheStrategicAdvisor.com.au or email

  support@TheStrategicAdvisor.com.au

ABOUT THE AUTHOR

Author, Business Coach, Business Entrepreneur & Property Investor

 Michael was born and raised in Cessnock in the NSW Hunter Valley.

He began buying and selling property in his early 20s. After leaving the military, he started his first business when he was 26 and has been building and selling businesses in multiple online and offline niches ever since.

A keen property investor, he and a business partner also bought over a dozen properties in a single year.

Michael once built a start-up business and sold it within nine months for a six-figure amount. In addition, he co-created the first trade services franchise in Australia.

This quote from Michael sums up his philosophy:

"Chances are the best time to sell something is when you don't want to. That's usually when it's looking its best, whether it be that shiny car you drive or a business making good money."

Michael is a lifelong student and practitioner of business, sales, marketing and psychology. He has travelled the world for both personal and professional development learning from many great mentors like Tony Robbins, Zig Ziglar, Robert Kiyosaki, Jay Abraham, Bill Glazer, Brian Tracey, Ted Nicholas, Michael Gerber, Bruce Lipton and Rich Schefren, in countries such as the USA, Canada, Mexico, China, Singapore, Hong Kong, the Philippines, Malaysia, Indonesia, Thailand, Vanuatu and New Caledonia to name just a few.

Michael is also a qualified clinical hypnotherapist. He overcame his stage fright fears using hypnotherapy. He successfully applies what he has learned in both his personal and professional lives.

He is passionate about working with the business owner first and then the business second, as he believes the business owner's limiting beliefs hold back the business's success.

In his spare time, Michael enjoys nothing more than a day out on the boat with family and friends on the beautiful Gold Coast Broadwater in Queensland, Australia. He has two daughters and a very hairy ragdoll cat named Ollie.

Ingram Content Group Australia Pty Ltd
Printed in Australia
AUHW010450260623
379949AU00008B/8